Victim Mee

Victim Meets Offender: The Impact of Restorative Justice and Mediation

by

Mark S. Umbreit

with

Robert B. Coates and Boris Kalanj

CRIMINAL JUSTICE PRESS

Willow Tree Press, Inc.

Monsey, New York

1994

Library of Congress Cataloging-in-Publication Data

Umbreit, Mark, 1949-
    Victim meets offender : the impact of restorative justice and mediation / by Mark S. Umbreit with Robert B. Coates and Boris Kalanj.
        p.   cm.
    Includes bibliographical references.
    ISBN 1-881798-02-X : $25.00
    1. Reparation—United States. 2. Mediation—United States.
3.Victims of crime—United States.   I. Coates, Robert B.
II. Kalanj, Boris. III. Title.
HV8688.U53   1994
364.6'8—dc20

                                                            94-4818
                                                            CIP

Contents

List of Tables and Figures vii

About the Author ix

Preface xi

1. Restorative Justice and Mediation: Is the Public Interested ? 1

2. What Have We Learned from Previous Studies 15

3. Evaluation of Four Programs in the U.S. 29

4. Program Sites and Participants 43

5. Immediate Outcomes of Mediation 61

6. Quality of Justice Impact: Client Satisfaction and
   Perceptions of Fairness 75

7. Quality of Justice Impact: Themes that Emerged
   from Victims and Offenders

   Written by Boris Kalanj 91

8. Mid-Range Outcomes: Restitution Completion
   and Recidivism 109

9. Mediation Observations: Case Examples and Analysis

   Written by Robert B. Coates 119

10. Issues to Be Faced in Starting
    a Local Program 139

11. Conclusions and Implications 153

References 169

List of Written / Audiovisual Resources:
Victim-Offender Mediation 175

continued

APPENDICES

1. Research Plan for Cross-Site Analysis
   of Victim-Offender Mediation 179

2. Cost Implications of Victim-Offender
   Mediation Programs 181

3. Parental Involvement in Victim-Offender
   Mediation

   Written by Boris Kalanj 187

4. Burglary Case Study 195

5. Stakeholder Analysis Form 205

6: Sample Victim Information Letter 207

7. Program Evaluation Kit:
   Victim-Offender Mediation Programs 209

List of Tables and Figures

Table 1: Paradigms of Justice—Old and New 3

Figure 1: International Development of Victim-Offender
Mediation 5

Figure 2: Public Support for Sentencing Burglar 10

Figure 3: Public Support for Crime Prevention 11

Figure 4: Support for Victim-Offender Mediation 12

Table 2: Samples for Individuals Interviewed 33

Table 3: Characteristics of Victim Samples 34

Table 4: Characteristics of Offender Samples 35

Table 5: 1991 Program Characteristics 55

Table 6: Offender Characteristics (1990-91) 56

Table 7: Referral Characteristics (1990-91) 56

Table 8: Reasons for Non-Participation in Mediation 59

Figure 5: Proportion of Referrals Resulting in a Mediation
Session 62

Figure 6: Number of Mediations Per Site 64

Figure 7: Successfully Negotiated Restitution Agreements 65

Figure 8: Frequency In Which Type of Restitution Appears in
Agreements 66

Figure 9: Average Amount of Financial Restitution Per
Negotiated Agreement 67

Figure 10: Average Amount of Personal Service Restitution
Per Agreement 68

Figure 11: Average Amount of Community Service Restitution
Per Agreement 69

Table 9: Immediate Outcomes (1990-91) 70

Table 10: Emotional Impact of Mediation on Victim 71

Table 11: Victim Attitudes About Important Issues 72

Table 12: Offenders' Attitudes About Important Issues 73

Figure 12: Victim Satisfaction 76

Figure 13: Victim Satisfaction By Site 77

Figure 14: Offender Satisfaction 78

Figure 15: Offender Satisfaction By Site 80

continued

Figure 16: Satisfaction With Outcome of Mediation Session 80

Figure 17: Satisfaction With Mediator 81

Figure 18: Ranking of Thoughts About Fairness 83

Figure 19: Victim Fairness Perceptions 84

Figure 20: Offender Fairness Perceptions 85

Figure 21: Offender Fairness Perceptions By Site 85

Figure 22: Victim Fairness Perceptions By Site 86

Figure 23: Fairness of Restitution Agreement to Victim in
Mediation 87

Figure 24: Fairness of Restitution Agreement to the Offender
in Mediation 88

Figure 25: Fairness of Mediator 89

Figure 26: Restitution Completion 111

Table 13: Restitution Completion By Offenders 112

Table 14: Characteristics of Minneapolis Mediation Sample
and Matched Comparison Sample 113

Table 15: Dollar Completion of Restitution Within One Year 114

Figure 27: Recidivism Analysis 115

Table 16: Seriousness of Recidivism 116

Table 17: Cost of Victim-Offender Mediation Programs 182

Table 18: Minneapolis Program Costs 183

Table 19: Oakland Program Costs 184

Table 20: Albuquerque Program Costs 185

Table 21: Parental Presence in Mediation Session 189

About the Author

Mark S. Umbreit

Mark S. Umbreit, Ph.D joined the faculty of the graduate School of Social Work at the University of Minnesota in the fall of 1990. Prior to this, he had worked with community correctional agencies and mediation programs for the PACT Institute of Justice in Valparaiso, IN and the Minnesota Citizens Council on Crime and Delinquency in Minneapolis. Dr. Umbreit is a nationally recognized trainer, mediator, author and researcher in the field of restorative justice and mediation, with more than 20 years' experience as a practitioner. As a consultant for the U.S. Department of Justice, Dr. Umbreit has provided technical assistance and training related to the development of mediation programs in nearly 30 states of the U.S. He is currently conducting the first cross-national study of victim-offender mediation in four provinces of Canada, two cities in England and four cities in the U.S. Dr. Umbreit has trained many hundreds of mediators in North America, and is the author of numerous articles and monographs, including his book *Crime and Reconciliation: Creative Options for Victims and Offenders.*

*Dedicated to Alexa,
Jenni, and Laura,
the most special people
in my life.*

Preface

This book is based largely upon a two-and-one-half-year study of victim-offender mediation programs in California, Minnesota, New Mexico and Texas. The research was made possible by a grant from the State Justice Institute in Alexandria, VA to the Minnesota Citizens Council on Crime and Justice in Minneapolis. The Minnesota Citizens Council on Crime and Justice contracted with the University of Minnesota for the services of the principal investigator.

A study of this magnitude is simply not possible without the active assistance of many individuals. A special thanks to Robert Coates, who served as the senior research associate and authored one of the following chapters, and Boris Kalanj, who served as the Senior Research Assistant and also authored a chapter. The support and guidance of John Clarke, John Conbere, Burt Galaway, Barbara Schmidt and Sue Wiese, as members of the Research Advisory Committee, were greatly appreciated. The leadership and support of Richard Ericson, President, and numerous other staff of the Minnesota Citizens Council on Crime and Justice were vital to the success of the research. The assistance provided by juvenile court officials, as well as program staff and volunteer mediators at the various program sites, was invaluable. Data collection and analysis would not have been possible without the valuable and much appreciated contribution of my numerous research assistants: Madeline Brown, Andy Galaway, Deborah Johnson, Boris Kalanj, Autumn Riddle, Sarah Orrick, Mike Schumacher, Laurie Smith, Becki Tovar and Cynthia Wright. The restitution completion analysis reported in this study is based, in part, upon the methodology developed by Andy Galaway in a prior smaller study of cases at the Minneapolis program site. Dale Jore provided helpful assistance with copy editing. The ongoing support of Dana Farthing Capowich at the State Justice Institute in Alexandria, VA, which provided the primary grant to support this research, was greatly appreciated. Thanks is also due to the Hewlett Foundation in California for providing matching funds to support this study, and to the Conflict and Change Center at the University of Minnesota for providing funds to allow the Austin, TX site to be added to this study.

Mark S. Umbreit, Ph.D.
November 1993

1. Restorative Justice and Mediation: Is the Public Interested?

Linda and Bob Jackson had their house broken into while they were away visiting friends in another city. The frustration, anger, and growing sense of vulnerability they felt far exceeded the loss of their television set and stereo. The young person, Allan, who committed this crime was caught and entered a plea of guilty. When the Jacksons were invited to participate in a program that allowed them to meet their offender, they were eager to get answers to questions such as "why us?" and "were you watching our movements?" The mediation session allowed them to get answers to these and other questions, let Allan know how personally violated they felt and negotiate a plan for him to pay them back. While nervous at first, Allan felt better after the mediation. Everyone treated him with respect even though he had committed a crime, and he was able to make amends to the Jacksons. Linda and Bob felt less vulnerable, were able to sleep better and received payment for their losses. All parties were able to put this event behind them.

The Jacksons are among many thousands of people who have been victimized and have been given the opportunity to experience a radically different way of "doing justice." Through their participation in a victim-offender mediation program, they were able to experience firsthand what the emerging theory of restorative justice is about.

Our contemporary understanding of social theory related to crime and victimization can be traced back to a major paradigm shift that occurred during the Norman invasion of Britain in the twelfth century. This marked a turning away from viewing crime as a victim-offender conflict within the context of community. Crime became a violation of the king's peace, and upholding the authority of the state replaced the practice of making the victim whole.

One of the most significant current developments in our thinking about crime is the growing interest in restorative justice theory (Mackey, 1990; Umbreit, 1993a, 1991b; Umbreit and Coates, 1993; Van Ness, 1986; Van Ness et al., 1989; Wright, 1991; Wright and Galaway, 1989; Zehr, 1990,

1985; Marshall and Merry, 1990; Galaway and Hudson, 1990; Messmer and Otto, 1992), which is based upon principles that were widely practiced prior to the Norman invasion of Britain. At a time in modern society when the current paradigm of justice has demonstrated very little positive impact on offenders, crime victims or the larger community, it is understandable that a promising theory of criminal justice is increasingly being embraced in a growing number of communities throughout the world.

Restorative justice theory provides an entirely different theoretical framework for responding to crime. Rather than defining "the state" as the victim, restorative justice theory postulates that criminal behavior is first a conflict between individuals. The person who was violated is the primary victim, and the state is a secondary victim. The current retributive paradigm of justice focuses on the actions of the offender, denies victim participation and requires only passive participation by the offender. The very definition of "holding offenders accountable" changes when viewed through the lens of restorative justice. As Zehr (1990) notes: "Instead of 'paying a debt to society' by experiencing punishment, accountability would mean understanding and taking responsibility for what has been done and taking action to make things right. Instead of owing an abstract debt to society, paid in an abstract way by experiencing punishment, the offender would owe a debt to the victim, to be repaid in a concrete way."

Restorative justice places both victim and offender in active problem-solving roles that focus upon the restoration of material and psychological losses to individuals and the community following the damage that results from criminal behavior. Whenever possible, dialogue and negotiation serve as central elements of restorative justice. This is true primarily of property crimes, although also of a growing number of more violent offenses. Problem solving for the future is seen as more important than establishing blame for past behavior. Public safety is a primary concern, yet severe punishment of the offender is less important than providing opportunities to: empower victims in their search for closure and healing; impress upon the offender the human impact of their behavior; and promote restitution to the victim.

By far the clearest distinction between the old paradigm of retributive justice and the new paradigm of restorative justice has been developed by Zehr (1990), as outlined in Table 1.

While clearly more difficult to apply in violent crimes, the principles of restorative justice theory are having an increasing impact on social policy. Many of these principles can also be seen in the pioneering work of an

Australian scholar who addresses the issues of crime, shame and reintegration. Braithwaite (1989) argues for "reintegrative shaming," a type of social control based upon informal community condemnation of wrongdoing, but with opportunities for the reintegration of the wrongdoer back into the community. He states that the most effective crime control requires active community participation "in shaming offenders, and, having shamed them, through concerted participation in...integrating the offender back into the community" (Braithwaite, 1989). Braithwaite notes that societies with low crime rates consist of people who do not mind their own business, where there exist clear limits to tolerance of deviance and where communities have a preference for handling their own problems.

While Braithwaite does not specifically address restorative justice or victim-offender mediation, he argues for principles of justice which emphasize personal accountability of offenders, active community involve-

Table 1: Paradigms of Justice—Old and New

Old Paradigm	New Paradigm
1. Crime defined as violation of state.	1. Crime defined as violation of one person by another.
2. Focus on establishing blame based on guilt, on past (did he/she do it?).	2. Focus on problem solving, on liabilities/obligations, on future (what should be done?).
3. Adversarial relationship and process are normative.	3. Dialogue and negotiation are normative.
4. Imposition of pain to punish and deter/prevent future crime.	4. Restitution as means of restoring both parties; goal of reconciliation/restoration.
5. Justice defined by intent and process: right rules.	5. Justice defined as right relationships; judged by outcome.
6. Interpersonal, conflictual nature of crime obscured, repressed; conflict seen as individual versus the state.	6. Crime recognized as interpersonal conflict; value of conflict is recognized.

Old Paradigm	New Paradigm
7. One social injury replaced by another.	7. Focus on repair of social injury.
8. Community on sidelines, represented abstractly by state.	8. Community as facilitator in restorative process.
9. Encouragement of competitive, individualistic values.	9. Encouragement of mutuality.
10. Action directed from state to offender - victim ignored, - offender passive.	10. Victim and offender's roles recognized in problem/solution: - victim rights/needs recognized, - offender encouraged to take responsibility.
11. Offender accountability defined as taking punishment.	11. Offender accountability defined as understanding impact of action, and helping to decide how to make things right.
12. Offense defined in purely legal terms, devoid of moral, social, economic, political dimensions.	12. Offense understood in whole context—moral, social, economic, political.
13. "Debt" owed to state and society in the abstract.	13. Debt/liability to victim recognized.
14. Response focused on offender's past behavior.	14. Response focused on harmful consequences of offender's behavior.
15. Stigma of crime unremovable.	15. Stigma of crime removable through restorative action.
16. No encouragement for repentance and forgiveness.	16. Possibilities for repentance and forgiveness.
17. Dependence upon proxy by professionals.	17. Direct involvement by participants.

Reprinted with permission from Howard Zehr.

ment, and a process of reconciliation and reaffirmation of the offender that directly relates to the restorative justice paradigm.

VICTIM-OFFENDER MEDIATION

The clearest expression of restorative justice theory is seen in the emerging field of victim-offender mediation (Fagan and Gehm, 1993; Galaway, 1989, 1988; Galaway and Hudson, 1990; Umbreit, 1993a, 1986a; Zehr, 1990, 1980). Developed extensively in recent years, it represents one of the most creative efforts to: hold offenders personally accountable for their behavior; emphasize the human impact of crime; provide opportunities for offenders to take responsibility for their actions by facing their victim and making amends; promote active victim and community involvement in the justice process; and enhance the quality of justice experienced by both victims and offenders. There are more than 120 victim-offender mediation programs in the U.S., 26 in Canada and an even larger number in Europe (Umbreit, 1991b), as noted in Figure 1.

Figure 1: International Development of Victim-Offender Mediation

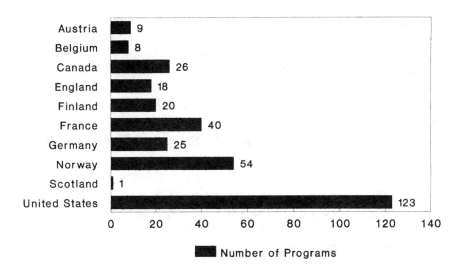

Number of Programs

Austria has a federal policy making victim-offender mediation available for youths in any of its 143 cities, within its 9 provinces.

A widespread network of victim-offender mediation programs is now developing throughout the U.S., Canada, England, Germany, France, Austria, Norway and Finland. While interest in restorative justice theory has grown extensively throughout North America and Europe, there exists a significant lack of empirical research to assess the impact of the theory.

The ultimate strength of any social theory is to be found in how accurately it captures the reality of people who are subject to it. Restorative justice theory makes bold claims about the needs of people affected by crime within community structures. Its validity as a new social theory must be grounded in empirical evidence offered by those most affected by crime—victims and offenders. Should restorative justice fail to become a "grounded theory" (Glazer and Strauss, 1967) from the bottom up, it risks the likelihood of becoming an abstraction—a philosophical exercise in criminal justice policy reform with little relevance to the reality of how justice is actually done in a free and democratic society. On the other hand, a grounded theory of restorative justice contains the powerful and prophetic potential for a fundamental change in how society understands and responds to crime in the community.

This book will offer such empirical grounding for the theory of restorative justice. It will report on the largest and most extensive multi-site analysis of victim-offender mediation to occur in North America (Umbreit, 1991a, 1993b; Umbreit and Coates, 1992, 1993). Over a two-and-one-half-year period, victim-offender mediation programs working with the juvenile courts in Albuquerque (NM), Austin (TX), Minneapolis (MN) and Oakland (CA) were examined. A total of 1,153 pre- and post-mediation interviews with victims and offenders were conducted. Two different comparison groups were used to examine the impact of mediation, along with numerous interviews with court officials and program staff, a review of court and program records, and 28 observations of actual mediation sessions.

The conclusions that emerged from this multi-site study, as will be noted in the final chapter, are consistent with a growing body of literature, particularly two recent studies conducted in England (Dignan, 1990; Marshall and Merry, 1990). Together, these studies provide important empirical evidence to support the basic propositions put forth by the restorative justice paradigm.

THE MEDIATION PROCESS

Victim-offender mediation and reconciliation programs differ in a variety of ways related to referral source, diversion versus post-adjudication referral, case management procedures, use of volunteer mediators, etc. A basic case management process, however, tends to be present in most of the programs in the U.S. and Canada, particularly those that have been influenced by the VORP (Victim Offender Reconciliation Program) model (Umbreit, 1988).

Nearly all victim-offender mediation and reconciliation programs focus upon providing a conflict resolution process that is perceived as fair to both parties. It is the mediator's responsibility to facilitate this process. First, the parties are given time to address informational and emotional needs. Once questions have been answered and feelings expressed, the mediation session then turns to a discussion of losses and the possibility of developing a mutually agreeable restitution plan (i.e., money, work for victim, work for victim's choice of a charity, etc.).

The process typically begins when judges, probation staff, prosecutors or victim assistance staff refer juvenile or adult offenders (most often those convicted of such crimes as theft and burglary) to the victim-offender mediation program. Many programs accept referrals after a formal admission of guilt has been entered with the court. Some programs accept cases that are referred prior to formal admission of guilt, as part of a deferred prosecution or diversion effort. Each case is then assigned to either a staff or volunteer mediator. Prior to scheduling the mediation session, the mediator meets with both the offender and victim separately. These individual meetings with each party play a very important role in the mediation process. The mediator listens to the story of each party, explains the program and encourages their participation.

Usually mediators meet first with the offender. If he or she is willing to proceed with mediation, they meet later with the victim. In addition to collecting information about the criminal event and explaining the program, these individual meetings provide an opportunity for the mediator to build rapport and trust with the individuals involved. Particularly since both parties are likely to have already been dealt with in an impersonal fashion by a variety of criminal justice officials, having the mediator meet with both individually before even scheduling the mediation is extremely important. It tends to humanize the justice process and result in a higher "getting-to-the-table" rate of actual mediation participation. These preliminary meetings, held separately with victims and offenders, require effective listening and communication skills. They are critical to building rapport and trust with both parties.

While crime victims are encouraged to consider the possible benefits of mediation, they must not be coerced into participating. To do so, even with the best of intentions, would be to revictimize them. Voluntary participation by crime victims and offenders—although for offenders it is a choice within a highly coercive context—is a strong ethical principle of the victim-offender mediation process. Presenting the mediation process as an option helps victims and offenders to feel empowered.

Program literature in the field implies that offender participation in the mediation process is also totally voluntary. Actual practice suggests something quite different. A rather significant amount of state coercion is exercised when offenders are ordered to participate in mediation by the court, via probation, or are diverted from prosecution if they complete the program. One early study (Coates and Gehm, 1985) found that offenders certainly did not perceive the process as voluntary. A more recent and much larger study (Umbreit and Coates, 1992, 1993), as will be reported in this book, found the vast majority of offenders believed they had a choice as to whether to participate in mediation.

A more honest approach is used by programs that attempt to secure offender participation in the least coercive manner possible. Offenders who are strongly opposed to participating are allowed to bow out of the program, while those who are determined by the program staff to be inappropriate for mediation are referred back to the referral source.

Once the victim and offender have indicated their willingness to participate, the mediator then schedules a face-to-face meeting. The mediation session begins with the mediator explaining his or her role, stating any communication ground rules that may be necessary, and stating the agenda for the meeting (first to talk about what happened and how they felt about it, and then to discuss losses and negotiate restitution).

During the first part of the mediation session, the focus is on the facts and feelings related to the crime. Crime victims are given the unusual opportunity to express their feelings directly to the person who violated them. They can get answers to questions such as "why me?", "how did you get into our house?", and "were you stalking us and planning on coming back?" Upon seeing their offender, victims are often relieved. This "criminal" usually bears little resemblance to the frightening character they may have conjured up in their minds.

Facing the person they violated is not easy for most offenders. While it is often an uncomfortable position for offenders, they are given the equally unusual opportunity to display a more human dimension to their character. For many, the opportunity to express remorse in a very direct and personal fashion is important. The mediation process allows victims and offenders to deal with each other as people, oftentimes from the same neighborhood, rather than as stereotypes and objects.

When both parties have concluded discussing the crime and how they felt about it, the second part of the meeting is then initiated. The losses incurred by the victim are reviewed, and a plan for making things right is discussed. The principles of fairness and realism are emphasized during the final negotiation of the restitution agreement. When courts refer cases to mediation, they do not usually order a specific restitution amount. Cases in which the parties are unable to agree upon the amount or form of restitution are referred back to the referral source, with a good likelihood that the offender will be placed in a different program. Mediators do not impose a restitution settlement.

Most programs report that in more than 95% of all mediation sessions a written restitution agreement has been successfully negotiated and signed by the victim, offender and mediator. Joint victim-offender meetings usually last about one hour, with some meetings in the two-hour range.

It is important to note that there exist a number of significant exceptions to the "typical" process described, particularly among many community dispute resolution centers that have mediated quite a few disputes among crime victims and offenders, but that did not frame the mediation as a "victim-offender mediation." For example, many of these community dispute resolution centers would have staff be responsible for all of the case development work, including any separate meetings or conversations with the parties prior to mediation. The mediator would first meet the victim and offender at the time of the mediation session.

IS THE PUBLIC INTERESTED?

Even in view of the empirical evidence in support of restorative justice theory and mediation to be offered in this book, the question remains "Is the larger public really interested?" Certainly the data that have emerged from examination of a number of individual programs are rather persuasive. Yet is there evidence of public support for the principles of restorative justice? The strong "law-and-order" and "get-tough" rhetoric that dominates most political campaigns would suggest not. After all, how often have we heard ambitious politicians or criminal justice officials state that "the public demands that we get tougher with criminals"? This perception—or some would argue, misperception—fuels the engine that drives our nation toward ever-increasing and costly criminal punishments, as seen in lengthy sentences and the highest per capita incarceration in the world (Mauer, 1991).

There is, however, a growing body of evidence to suggest that the general public is far less vindictive than often portrayed and far more supportive of the basic principles of restorative justice than many might think. A recent statewide public opinion survey, conducted by the University of Minnesota (Pranis and Umbreit, 1992) using a large probability sample, challenges conventional wisdom about public feelings related to crime and punishment.

A sample of 825 Minnesota adults, demographically and geographically balanced to reflect the state's total population, were asked three questions with implications for restorative justice as part of a larger omnibus survey. A sampling of this size has a sampling error of plus or minus 3.5 percentage points. The first question was: "Suppose that while you are away, your home is burglarized and $1,200 worth of property is stolen.

Figure 2: Public Support for Sentencing Burglar

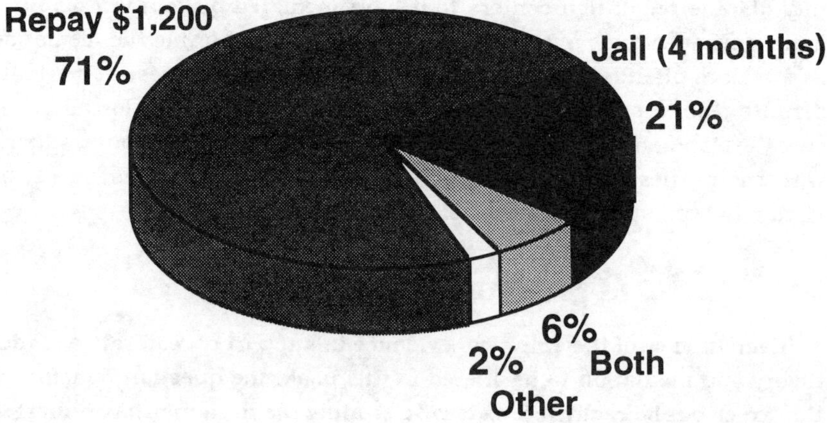

Minnesota State sample, 1991

"The burglar has one previous conviction for a similar offense. In addition to 4 years on probation, would you prefer the sentence include repayment of $1,200 to you or 4 months in jail?" Nearly three of four Minnesotans indicated that having the offender pay restitution was more important than a jail sentence, as indicated in Figure 2.

To examine public support for policies that address some of the underlying social problems that often cause crime, a concern that is closely related to restorative justice, the following question was asked: "For the greatest impact on reducing crime, should additional money be spent on more prisons, or spent on education, job training and community programs?" Spending on education, job training and community programs rather than on prisons to reduce crime was favored by four of five Minnesotans, as seen in Figure 3.

Figure 3: Public Support for Crime Prevention

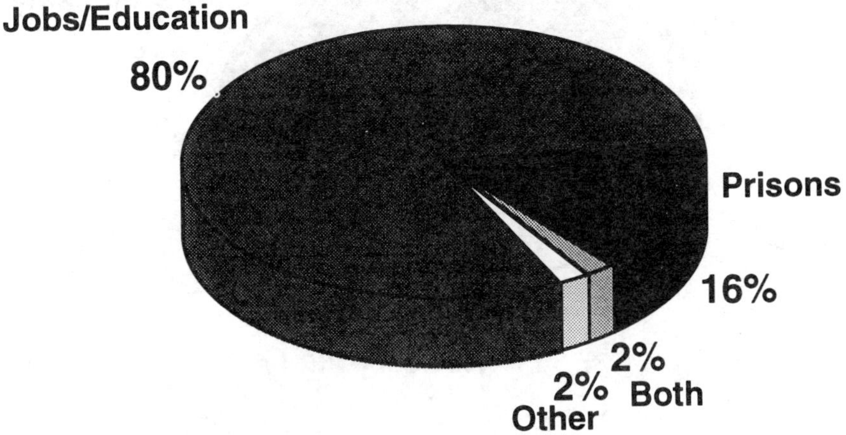

Jobs/Education
80%

Prisons

16%

2%
2% Both
Other

Minnesota State sample, 1991

The third and final question related to restorative justice addressed the issue of interest in victim-offender mediation. This question was presented in the following manner: "Minnesota has several programs which allow crime victims to meet with the person who committed the crime, in the presence of a trained mediator, to let this person know how the crime affected them, and to work out a plan for repayment of losses. Suppose you were the victim of a non-violent property crime committed by a juvenile or young adult. How likely would you be to participate in a program like this?"

More than four of five Minnesotans expressed an interest in participating in a face-to-face mediation session with the offender. This finding is particularly significant in that criminal justice officials and program staff who are unfamiliar with mediation often make such comments as "there is no way in the world that victims in my community would ever want to confront the offender," or "only a small portion of victims would ever be interested." The finding is particularly important since the vast majority of crime is committed by either juveniles or young adults. Some would suggest that the victim-offender mediation process is likely to be supported only for crimes involving juvenile offenders. This is certainly not the case in Minnesota. As noted in Figure 4, 82% of respondents indicated

Figure 4: Support for Victim-Offender Mediation

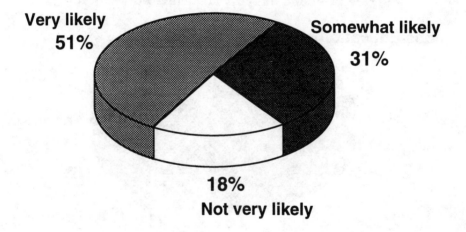

Very likely
51%

Somewhat likely
31%

18%
Not very likely

Minnesota State sample, 1991

they would be likely to participate in a program that would allow them to meet the juvenile or young adult who victimized them.

A picture of a far less vindictive public than often portrayed emerges from this statewide survey. Respondents indicated greater concern for restitution and prevention strategies that address underlying issues of social injustice than for costly retribution. Holding offenders personally accountable to their victim is more important than incarceration in a jail. Public safety is understood to be more directly related to investing in job training, education and other community programs than incarceration.

While it might be tempting to suggest that this public opinion survey simply reflects the rather unique liberal social policy tradition of Minnesota, its findings are consistent with a growing body of public opinion research across the U.S. (Bae, 1991; Gottfredson, Warner and Taylor, 1988; Clark, 1985; Public Agenda Foundation, 1987,1989,1991; Public Opinion Research, 1986). These previous studies have found broad public support for payment of restitution by the offender to their victim instead of incarceration for property crimes, and support for crime prevention strategies instead of prison strategies to control crime. The studies did not explicitly ask respondents if they supported "restorative justice." The questions asked, however, addressed important underlying principles that are fundamental to the theory of restorative justice, which places far more value on crime prevention and restoration of physical and emotional losses than on retribution and blame for past behavior.

2. What We Have Learned from Previous Studies

- *High level of client satisfaction*
- *Mediation humanizes the justice process*
- *Over 90% of mediation sessions result in a successful negotiated restitution plan to compensate the victim*
- *High level of successful restitution completion*
- *Mediation process and outcome perceived as fair by both victims and offenders*

The growing practice of providing victims with the opportunity to confront their offender, in the presence of a third-party mediator, remains a relatively new criminal justice reform effort. By allowing victims and offenders to get answers to questions, express their feelings and negotiate mutually acceptable restitution agreements, the victim-offender mediation process focuses upon humanizing the justice process for both offenders and victims. Despite more than 15 years of program development in the U.S. and a network of more than 100 programs, there exist only a handful of empirical studies aimed at assessing the victim-offender mediation approach.

The purpose of this chapter is to review the major empirical studies of victim-offender mediation. While the focus will be upon studies conducted in the U.S., several other important research initiatives in Canada and England will also be noted. Key findings from each will be presented, major themes identified and implications for further research in this emerging field presented.

The first known controlled research project (Davis et al., 1980) assessing the impact of mediation upon cases referred by the criminal courts occurred in New York. Its focus was on a unique project in New York City that worked primarily with cases that arose from felony arrests, most often assault or burglary. This fact set apart the Brooklyn Dispute Resolution Center from the growing number of mediation and conflict resolution programs being established throughout the country, nearly all of which would not even consider cases of felony arrests. Sponsored jointly by the Institute for Mediation and Conflict Resolution in New York City and the

Victim/Witness Assistance Project of the VERA Institute of Justice, the Brooklyn Dispute Resolution Center mediated or arbitrated disputes between persons who knew each other that erupted into criminal offenses for which arrests were made. While not identifying itself as a "victim-offender mediation program," the mediation process was offered to the parties involved as a voluntary alternative to the conventional process of prosecution in Brooklyn Criminal Court.

An evaluation of this project by Davis and his colleagues (1980) compared the impact of mediation and prosecution on disputants' satisfaction with the process by which their cases were resolved. The recurrence of hostilities in their relationships was also examined. Cases involving arrests screened as appropriate for mediation were randomly assigned into control and experimental groups. The comparison of the groups revealed that complainants whose cases were referred to mediation felt they had greater opportunity to participate in resolution of the dispute, felt that the presiding official had been fairer, and felt that the outcome was more fair and more satisfactory. Similar responses were found among defendants. The research, however, found no indication that further conflict between the participants was less frequent in cases that entered mediation as opposed to formal court intervention.

While in some respects similar to programs identified as victim-offender mediation or reconciliation, the Brooklyn Dispute Resolution Center was also different in that all offenders referred to it were diverted from prosecution, and the parties involved had a continuing relationship. In victim-offender mediation programs, cases are referred either pre- or post-conviction, and few participants know each other prior to the offense.

It was not until 1974 that the specific intervention now called "victim-offender reconciliation" first began on the North American continent in a small experiment conducted in Kitchener, Ontario, CAN through the leadership of Mennonite Church representatives, and a local judge and probation officer. Contact between victims and offenders, however, had previously occurred in a number of programs, most notably the nationally recognized Minnesota Restitution Center in Minneapolis. Use of mediation at a pretrial diversion level had also occurred. However, the victim-offender reconciliation process represented a significant extension of these other efforts by applying structured mediation techniques in a systematic fashion with convicted offenders and their victims, usually involving the offenses of burglary and theft.

In general, the victims and offenders involved in the program had no prior relationship. Rather than a primary emphasis upon restitution collection, the initial Victim Offender Reconciliation Program (VORP) first emphasized the need to address the emotional and informational needs of both parties through the process of face-to-face mediation, with restitution representing an important additional goal. As one expression of the mediation process, the VORP model was not simply an offender rehabilitation program, nor was it only a victim assistance program. Rather, it was designed to address the needs of both victims and offenders by personalizing the process of justice and facilitating the empowerment of both parties to resolve the conflict at a community level (Umbreit, 1985, 1986a). The early success of the program in Kitchener quickly led to its replication in other parts of Canada.

The first replication of the VORP model in the U.S. occurred in 1978 in the northern Indiana community of Elkhart, once again through the leadership of Mennonite Church representatives, a local judge, several probation staff, as well as a local community corrections organization called PACT (Prisoner and Community Together). Within several years, the Elkhart project began receiving national and international attention from the criminal justice community (Umbreit, 1988).

The most informative initial study related to the impact of victim-offender mediation and reconciliation was conducted by Coates and Gehm (1989), who evaluated VORPs in four Indiana communities. The study represented the first major attempt to examine VORPs in the U.S. These VORPs received referrals of offenders from the courts, usually following conviction. A trained mediator would first meet separately with both parties to listen to their story, explain the program and encourage their participation. If both agreed to participate, the mediator would then bring the offender and the victim to a face-to-face meeting, during which time the victim could get answers to questions and could express concerns directly to the person that violated him or her. In addition, the offender had an opportunity to display a more human side to his or her character and was able to negotiate a restitution plan with the victim (Zehr and Umbreit, 1982).

Coates and Gehm (1989) found that for those who participated in the victim-offender reconciliation process, being responded to as persons— victims and offenders—was probably seen as the greatest strength of the program. While some victims initially became involved in the program to recoup their losses, they left the process feeling that they had been dealt with fairly and with dignity. Other findings include: offenders appeared to take the mediation process seriously and seemed to have a better sense that what they did hurt people and required a response; victims and justice officials placed a great deal of value on the increased participation of victims; restitution completion by offenders in mediation was high; both victims and offenders viewed the program as a legitimate form of punishment; and there was some evidence to suggest that VORP, in conjunction with some short local jail time, was being used as an alternative to more lengthy state incarceration in selected cases.

Satisfaction with the VORP experience was expressed by 83% of the offenders and 59% of the victims. Another 30% of victims were somewhat satisfied. Some level of dissatisfaction was expressed by only 11% of the victims, and much of this was related to not receiving full restitution rather than to the VORP meeting itself. If they had the opportunity to do it over again, 97% of the victims would still choose to participate in VORP. The same percentage of victims would recommend VORP to other victims of crime. All of the offenders would again choose to participate in VORP if they had a choice.

Victims identified the following elements as the most satisfying:

(1) the opportunity to meet the offender to obtain a better understanding of the crime and the offender's situation,

(2) the opportunity to receive payment for loss,

(3) the expression of remorse on the part of the offender, and

(4) the care and concern of the mediator.

The study notes that more victims commented on meeting with the offender than on restitution, even though the number-one reason most victims chose to participate in the first place was financial restitution. Aspects of the process that victims found least satisfying were:

(1) lack of adequate follow-up and leverage on the offender to fulfill the agreed-upon contract,

(2) the time delay from offense to actual resolution through the VORP process, and

(3) the amount of time required to participate in VORP.

From the offender's perspective, the most satisfying things about the process were:

(1) meeting the victim and discovering he or she was willing to listen to them,

(2) staying out of jail and, in some instances, not getting a record, and

(3) the opportunity to work out a realistic schedule for paying back the victim and "making things right."

The research found that an offender would often list meeting the victim as both the most and the least satisfying part of the experience. The study suggests that this probably reflects the tension between, on the one hand, the stress experienced in preparation for meeting the victim and, on the other hand, the sense of relief over having taken steps to make things right.

For both victims and offenders who participated in a face-to-face meeting, there was a very high probability that restitution contracts would be agreed upon (98%) and successfully completed (82% of financial and 90% of service restitution). In addition, 79% of the victims and 78% of the offenders believed that justice had been served in their cases.

Coates and Gehm (1989) conclude that VORP appears to be an effective means for increasing victim involvement in the criminal justice process. "The VORP process encourages personal accountability on the part of the offender while breaking down stereotypes of both offenders and victims. To the extent that it is desirable to personalize crime and justice, the VORP approach has much to offer."

THE "FAIRNESS" GOAL

While "fairness" is a major goal of the justice system, and of the theory and practice of victim-offender mediation, little is known about what fairness actually means to crime victims themselves. The concept of fairness as experienced by victims involved in the mediation process was examined by Umbreit (1989a, 1990). This study gathered data from 50 face-to-face interviews with victims of burglary committed by juveniles in Hennepin County, MN (Minneapolis area) who were referred to the Victim Offender Reconciliation Program of the Minnesota Citizens Council on Crime and Justice during 1986 and 1987. Sixty-two percent of the victims who were interviewed for the study participated in a mediation session with their offender. The remainder chose not to enter the mediation process, even though they were referred to VORP. Both qualitative and quantitative data were collected from all subjects. Although the findings cannot be generalized to a larger population, they do suggest important themes that may be present in other jurisdictions.

The dominant meaning of fairness to burglary victims in the study focused upon more of a "restorative" than a "retributive" sense of justice.

Three dimensions of fairness emerged from interviews with victims: punishment of the offender, compensation of the victim and rehabilitation of the offender. These dimensions were found for both victims who participated in mediation (62%) and for those who were referred to the program but who chose not to enter the mediation process (38%).

The most frequent and intense concern about fairness expressed by victims was related to rehabilitation services for the offender, such as counseling, family therapy or educational assistance. Both victims who participated in mediation (100%) and those who did not (90%) expressed this concern. Compensation of the victim through restitution was the second most frequent concern about fairness. Punishment of the offender through some type of incarceration was the least frequent concern about fairness.

The qualitative data derived from the open-ended questions allowed for construction of a typology of fairness consisting of three categories represented by the metaphors of "The Healer" (rehabilitation), "The Fixer" (compensation) and "The Avenger" (punishment). Participation by crime victims in the criminal justice process was found to be a major element of fairness across all categories of victims. The importance of victim participation in the justice process included both passive forms (information provision by letter) and active forms (court appearance and/or mediation).

Participants in the mediation process indicated a very high level of satisfaction: 97% felt they were treated fairly in the mediation session; 94% felt the mediator was fair; 93% felt the negotiated restitution agreement was fair; and 86% found it helpful to meet the offender, talk about the offense, and negotiate a plan for restitution.

A particularly significant finding of this study (Umbreit, 1989a, 1990) was that victims who were referred to the VORP and who participated in a mediation session with their offender were twice as likely to have experienced fairness (80%) regarding the manner in which the criminal justice system dealt with their case than victims who were referred to the VORP but who chose not to enter mediation (38%). Umbreit (1989a, 1990) notes that the client satisfaction data from this study would suggest that the mediation process, including an empowering style of mediation, employed by the VORP project in Minnesota contributes to crime victim experience of fairness, although the precise nature and degree of that contribution cannot be determined by the limitations of this study. The data from this study (Umbreit, 1989b, 1990) suggest that placing certain victims in a far more active role in the criminal justice process, including negotiating a portion of the penalty (restitution) incurred by their offender, may need broader consideration by criminal justice policymakers.

CLIENT SATISFACTION

Expanding upon his earlier study, Umbreit (1991c) examined issues related to client satisfaction and fairness for both victims and offenders involved in the Center for Victim Offender Mediation (CVOM) in Minneapolis, formerly known as VORP. This study was based upon post-mediation interviews with a sample of 51 victims and 66 juvenile offenders.

During 1989, a total of 379 cases were referred to the CVOM, representing 228 individual victims and 257 individual offenders. Because a case is defined as each victim-offender combination, one offender with three victims represents three cases. Of these referrals, 56% represented misdemeanor/gross misdemeanor offenses, and 44% were felony offenses. The most common offenses were vandalism (32%), theft (25%), burglary (15%) and tampering (11%). Other offenses included car theft (8%), assault (6%) and robbery (3%). Sixty-one percent of the referrals occurred post-adjudication, and 39% occurred as a diversion from adjudication.

Of the 379 cases referred to the CVOM in 1989, 50% resulted in face-to-face mediation; 9%, indirect mediation; and 41%, no mediation (involving referral back to the court for determining restitution). There were a number of reasons why cases did not enter the mediation process, including: victim was unwilling (35%); offender was unwilling (24%); the conflict was resolved by the parties prior to the court referral (17%); and one of the parties could not be located (10 %). Restitution agreements were reached in 96% of the mediation cases. These agreements included $23,328 of monetary restitution, 403 hours of personal service restitution for the victim, 787 hours of community service restitution and 17 agreements with only an apology required by the victim.

The data collected for this program evaluation indicate a high level of client satisfaction with the mediation process among both victims and offenders. Consistent with prior research (Coates and Gehm, 1989; Umbreit, 1989b, 1990), crime victims who met with their offenders in the mediation program (the CVOM) indicated that being able to meet the offender, talk about what happened, express their concerns and work out a restitution plan were more important than actually receiving compensation for their losses. While 3 of 4 victims stated that receiving restitution was important, 9 of 10 victims cited other, more important, non-monetary benefits. Also consistent with prior research, eight of ten victims were concerned about the offender's need for counseling and other rehabilitative services.

Three themes capture what crime victims liked the most about mediation. First, telling the offender how the crime affected them emotionally and/or financially was important. "It was a chance to tell the offender the hardship it put on us as a family." "It was important to just let him know what he put me through, that it was more than one person he victimized."

A second theme was the importance of being able to directly confront the offender. "I liked that the kid had to look me in the eyes." "I guess being able to meet him face to face and realize that he was just a kid who made a mistake was what I liked the most."

The third most common theme expressed by these victims addressed their concern for helping the very person who victimized them. "I wanted most of all to help the boy." "The program helps the offender make restitution, and I feel better knowing the person will get help." "Confronting their victims could straighten the kids out."

Crime victims had positive attitudes toward the actual mediation session and its outcome. Nine of ten victims felt good about being in the mediation program, and nearly all felt the restitution agreement was fair to both parties. Eighty-six percent of the victims indicated that meeting their offender was helpful, and the majority (55%) had a positive attitude toward their offender. Following the mediation, nine of ten (94%) victims experienced no fear of revictimization by their offender.

Victims who participated in the mediation were overwhelmingly satisfied with the program. The only things that several victims disliked about the program were the anticipatory anxiety they experienced prior to the meeting—"the unknown of the meeting, not knowing what they'd be like"—and the initial tension they experienced in the mediation session, as indicated by statements such as "I felt nervous" and "it was a very tense situation."

Juvenile offenders involved in the mediation services provided by the CVOM were also quite satisfied with the program. Telling the victim what happened, working out a mutually acceptable restitution plan, paying the victim back and apologizing were important issues to nine of ten offenders. Ninety-five percent of the offenders in this study actually offered an apology to their victim.

Offenders indicated a slightly lower level of satisfaction with their mediator and the outcome of the mediation than did their victims. Whereas 92% of victims indicated a positive attitude toward their mediator, 88% of the offenders did so. Similarly, whereas nearly all victims indicated that the actual restitution agreement was fair to both parties, 88% of offenders stated the agreement was fair to them, and 95% indicated it was fair to their victim. Ninety-four percent of the offenders felt it was helpful to meet their victim, 95% of the offenders felt better after meeting their victim, 84% believed their victim had a better opinion of them, and nearly all (96%) would suggest victim-offender mediation to a friend.

In response to open-ended questions about what offenders liked the most and the least about the mediation program, several themes emerged. Getting to know the victim, finding out that the victim was nice, and getting the victim to understand them constituted the most common themes expressed by the juvenile offenders. "He understood the mistake I made, and I really did appreciate him for it." "The victim was fair and nice about it." The positive quality of the communication between the offender and their victim was also a common theme. "I liked the honesty." "It was good to be able to actually say how you felt about it." "I liked that we could talk and get things out in the open."

Being able to apologize to their victim, having the chance to tell the victim what happened and working out a restitution plan were other important, but less frequent, themes expressed by some of the offenders.

What offenders disliked the most was the anxiety that many experienced prior to and during the meeting. "It was hard meeting him face to face." "It was kind of scary and nerve wracking." "Before I met him it was scary." "I didn't like the beginning of the meeting because you are so afraid." "I felt kind of stupid and guilty because he was real sad...but it felt better after I had a chance to apologize."

VICTIM PARTICIPATION IN VORP

Factors related to victim participation in mediation sessions with their offenders were examined by Gehm (1990). This exploratory study analyzed data from six victim-offender reconciliation programs located in Indiana, Minnesota, Oregon and Wisconsin. Three factors emerged as significantly affecting the victim's decision to participate in a mediation session with their offender. Gehm (1990) found that victims were more likely to enter the mediation process (face to face) if the offender was white, if the crime that was committed was a misdemeanor, and if the victim represented an institution such as a school or church as opposed to an individual victim. Even when controlling for the race and sex of the victim, the three above-mentioned factors held. Gehm (1990) notes, however, that these findings must be viewed as suggestive only since there were relatively few minority victims in the sample.

Gehm (1990) also looked at the issues of the frequency of actual meetings occurring between victims and offenders, the development of mutually agreeable restitution contracts, and successful completion of the agreed-upon restitution contract. The victim declined to participate in a meeting with their offender in 53% of the cases examined by Gehm (1990). Restitution agreements were negotiated between the victim and their offender in 91% of the cases that came to a mediation session, and 87% of those restitution agreements were successfully completed.

RECIDIVISM

The issue of recidivism among offenders who participated in a victim-offender mediation program in the U.S. has been directly addressed by only one known study, prior to the research reported in this book. While Guedalia (1979) found that contact with their victims was significantly related to a reduction in recidivism among juveniles offenders in Tulsa County, OK, the degree of "victim contact" was limited to simply meeting each other or exchanging a letter of apology; it did not include actual participation in a victim-offender mediation session.

Schneider (1986) found a significant reduction (from 63 to 53%) in recidivism among juvenile offenders in Washington, DC who were involved in a restitution program involving victim-offender mediation, as compared to offenders who were randomly assigned to regular probation supervision. Referrals to this program represented serious felony offenders, with more than 60% being repeat offenders. A complicating factor, however, was that even those offenders who were referred to mediation but chose not to participate (40%) had a lower recidivism rate than those offenders randomly assigned to regular probation. This finding suggests that even the rather minimal intervention of allowing juvenile offenders a choice in how they are processed by the courts has a positive effect on their future behavior. It is important to note that the mediation program in Washington, D.C. was considerably different from the victim-offender mediation programs reviewed in this report.

NATIONAL SURVEY

A final study worth noting is a national survey of victim-offender mediation programs conducted by Hughes and Schneider (1989). Questionnaire data were obtained from 79 of 171 programs that reported use of victim-offender mediation with juvenile offenders. The survey focused upon such program characteristics as program administration, characteristics of mediators and mediation, characteristics of the final contract and support for the mediation program.

The most important goals of victim-offender mediation, as expressed by those involved in the programs at some level, were ranked in the following order, from most to least important: 1) holding the offender accountable; 2) providing restitution; 3) making the victim whole; 4) reconciling victim and offender; 5) rehabilitating the offender; and 6) providing an alternative to incarceration. All of these goals were considered to be important. The additional goal of punishing the offender was rated as relatively unimportant.

Many of the mediation programs in the survey were administered by private, non-profit organizations, although some were operated directly by probation departments or other public agencies. In just over half of the programs, program staff alone were used as mediators, with nearly 40% using both program staff and volunteers. Fewer than 10% of the programs in the survey used only volunteer mediators.

The most often cited component of restitution agreements that were negotiated in a mediation session was monetary restitution. Components that were less frequently mentioned were community service, a combination of community service and monetary restitution, and behavioral requirements of the offender, such as school attendance or counseling.

The juvenile court judge was considered to be the most important support required to operate victim-offender mediation programs with juveniles. Other important elements of support were: parents and other family members; state juvenile service providers; city/county commissioners; public defenders; alternative juvenile program providers; law enforcement officials; prosecutors; local service organizations; and state officials (Hughes and Schneider, 1989).

Respondents indicated a uniformly positive response toward the effectiveness of mediation as both a specific program and a dispositional alternative. Even though the programs in the survey varied in age and size of jurisdiction, they were all similar in their basic structure.

In addition to the studies noted above, a handful of studies in Canada and England have been conducted during recent years. High levels of client satisfaction and perceptions of fairness with the victim-offender mediation process and outcome have been found in Canada (Collins, 1983, 1984; Fischer and Jeune, 1987; Perry, Lajeunesse and Woods, 1987) and in England (Marshall and Merry, 1990). The study by Marshall and Merry (1990) represents an extensive multi-site examination of the initial British experience in implementing victim-offender mediation programs, with many important implications for practitioners and policymakers.

An evaluation by the Attorney General's Office of Manitoba (Perry, Lajeunesse and Woods, 1987) of a large victim-offender mediation program in Winnipeg, operated by Mediation Services and sponsored by the Mennonite Central Committee, found that 92% of both complainants and respondents were satisfied with the mediation process and outcomes. It was also found that 81% of all interviewees would use the mediation program again if they were ever in the same situation.

Most of the above studies, however, had weak designs with no comparison groups. An evaluation of a victim-offender mediation program in England (Dignan, 1990) employed a quasi-experimental design, with a comparison group, and found client satisfaction levels consistent with the above studies. Two English studies (Marshall and Merry, 1990; Dignan, 1990) found marginal but non-significant reductions in recidivism.

Several studies, however, have identified some weaknesses in the victim-offender mediation model. A Canadian study (Dittenhoffer and Ericson, 1983) examined the systemic impact of such programs and found that, despite the rhetoric of program staff about mediation being an alternative to incarceration, there existed little evidence to support such a claim. This study did find, however, other values of the victim-offender reconciliation process—such as directly resolving conflict between the offender and victim— that could justify the VORP despite its lack of impact on serving as a substitute for the incarceration of certain offenders. A study of several programs in a midwestern state in the U.S. (Coates and Gehm, 1989) produced similar findings, although a small effect on reducing the length and location of incarceration (in local jails rather than state prisons) was found.

Based upon his examination of programs in England, Davis (1988) has been critical of victim-offender mediation because of his belief that the goal of diverting certain offenders from prosecution (as a result of participating in mediation) is fundamentally incompatible with the goal of offering reparation or restitution to the victim, particularly in the context of a retributive criminal justice system. It should be noted that many victim-offender mediation programs work with post-adjudication cases, as well as diversion cases.

IMPLICATIONS

The limited number of empirical studies that have examined victim-offender mediation have found rather favorable outcomes, including high levels of client satisfaction with the mediation process and perceptions of fairness (Coates and Gehm, 1989; Collins, 1983, 1984; Dignan, 1991; Fischer and Jeune, 1987; Marshall and Merry, 1990; Perry, Lajeunesse and Woods, 1987; Umbreit, 1989a, 1990, 1991c), and a positive impact upon recidivism (Schneider, 1986). However, these studies have some significant limitations.

Nearly all of the client satisfaction data reported in the studies were presented without examining their relationship to a comparison group of victims and offenders who did not participate in the mediation process. While it is helpful to know that a high level of client satisfaction existed among victims and offenders who participated in mediation, it would be far more enlightening to know if client satisfaction with mediation was significantly different from satisfaction with the normal court process in which mediation did not occur.

Though the Guedalia study (1979) and the Schneider study (1986) found some positive impact of victim-offender contact upon recidivism, neither study clearly indicates the impact of the mediation process specifically. In the Guedalia study, only relatively brief contact between the victim and the offender was examined. In the Schneider (1986) study, it was not clear whether the offender's willingness to participate in a mediation process was the most significant factor in recidivism reduction, rather than actual participation in mediation.

In the coming years it will be important to further examine issues related to client satisfaction and perceptions of fairness through the use of comparison groups that are matched along important variables such as age, race, sex, offense, and prior involvement with the courts. The issue of actual restitution completion by offenders who went through the mediation process, as compared to similar offenders who were ordered by the court to pay restitution, will also need to be thoroughly examined.

Finally, further examination of future criminal behavior by those offenders who participated in a victim-offender mediation program is important. Such an analysis should include multiple measures of recidivism in order to determine the frequency, intensity and severity of any further criminal behavior.

3. Evaluation of Four Programs in the U.S.

- *Quasi-experimental design*
- *Two comparison groups*
- *Completion of 1,153 interviews*
- *Pre- and post-mediation interviews*
- *Program sites in four states*

In order to conduct a cross-site analysis of programs that apply mediation techniques to resolve conflict between crime victims and offenders, a great deal of negotiation was required with program staff and juvenile justice officials. The goal was to gain access to data and develop research procedures that did not interfere with the day-to-day operation of the programs. Development of common interview schedules that were both meaningful and appropriate across all four sites in different geographical and cultural settings was particularly important. Without the ability to apply a collaborative model of field research with practitioners, this large multi-site study of victim-offender mediation would not have been possible.

A true experimental design, with random assignment of subjects into experimental and control groups, was considered but rejected for both ethical and practical reasons that research and program staff agreed upon. Therefore, a quasi-experimental design, with two comparison groups, was employed. The 1,153 interviews completed during calendar year 1990 and 1991 with victims and offenders were based upon availability samples at all four of the program sites. The study is based primarily upon a thorough examination of three victim-offender mediation programs located in Albuquerque (NM), Minneapolis (MN) and Oakland (CA). A fourth program, in Austin (TX), was added much later in the study and received a more limited range of analysis.

The three primary programs are operated by private, non-profit, community-based organizations that work closely with the courts. The cases involve juvenile offenders who are involved primarily in property crimes and who are referred by the local courts and probation staff.

These sites were selected for several reasons. The majority of victim-offender mediation programs throughout the country are operated by private, non-profit organizations and focus primarily upon juvenile offenders (Umbreit 1986a, 1988). Together, the three primary program sites offered not only regional diversity but also program development diversity. While they employed a very similar process with juvenile offenders and their victims, each had a different level of programmatic maturity and experience. Permission was obtained from the directors of each program to have access to records related to the study group and to be able to contact subjects.

A fourth site in Austin, TX was added late in the study. This program is operated by the Travis County Juvenile Court Department, in conjunction with the local dispute resolution center. Precisely because all of the initial three sites were sponsored by private agencies, the Austin program offered a unique addition to the original design of the study, by allowing for analysis of any possible effects of a public-versus-private victim-offender mediation program upon client satisfaction and perceptions of fairness.

The study made use of six main data sets at each of the three primary sites in Albuquerque, Minneapolis and Oakland. These included:

EXPERIMENTAL GROUP:

(1) Victims who participated in mediation.

(2) Offenders who participated in mediation.

COMPARISON GROUP #1:

(1) Victims who were referred to mediation but did not participate.

(2) Offenders who were referred to mediation but did not participate.

COMPARISON GROUP #2:

(1) Victims from the same jurisdiction who were never referred to mediation, and whose offenders were matched along several variables with offenders in the mediation sample.

(2) Offenders from the same jurisdiction who were never referred to mediation, and who were matched along the variables of age, sex, race and offense with offenders in the mediation sample.

At the Austin site, only two samples were examined. This occurred because the Austin site was added late in the study and with a limited amount of resources available to pay for the cost of interviews. Only the two experimental-group samples of victims and offenders who participated in mediation were interviewed.

Interviews were conducted at pre-mediation (usually within a week of the mediation) and post-mediation (approximately two months after the mediation). The comparison-group interviews were conducted approximately two months after the case disposition date. Only post-mediation interviews were conducted at the Austin site. The majority of post-mediation interviews at all four sites were in person and lasted between 45 and 60 minutes, on average. If an in-person interview was not possible, a telephone interview was conducted; this occurred in only a small number of cases. All of the other interviews (pre-mediation and all comparison-group interviews) utilized a briefer instrument and were conducted over the phone. In addition to the interviews with victims and offenders, data were gathered from 28 observations of mediations across the three primary program sites, and from interviews with program and probation staff and judges.

This study employed both quantitative and qualitative research techniques. Some research questions, such as those related to program cost issues, recidivism and restitution completion rates, required quantitative research techniques. As an exploratory study designed to gain a more thorough understanding of the impact of victim-offender mediation, the use of open-ended questions, with probes, was essential to address some of the research questions. A number of Likert scales were also used, and descriptive statistics related to respondent characteristics were collected. Structured interview schedules consisting of both closed-ended (including Likert scales) and open-ended questions were employed.

RESEARCH QUESTIONS

The study was guided by the following questions:

(1) Who participates in the victim-offender mediation process and why?

(2) How does the mediation process actually work, and what is the nature of the mediator's role and function?

(3) How do participants evaluate the mediation process?

(4) What do court officials think about the mediation process?

(5) What are the immediate outcomes of the mediation process?

(6) To what extent is successful completion of restitution by the offender affected by the mediation process?

(7) To what extent is recidivism affected by the mediation process?

(8) What are the cost implications of operating mediation programs?

(9) What is the meaning of fairness to victims and offenders participating in the mediation process?

REFERRAL TO MEDIATION SAMPLES

Participants in Mediation Referrals

All victims and offenders referred to the three primary mediation
programs during 1990 and 1991 were given the opportunity to participate
in the study. A total of 532 participants (see Table 2) in mediation
participated in the study, representing approximately 24% of the total
participants in mediations held during this time period. There were no
major differences in the characteristics of victims and offenders in mediation who were in the study and those who chose not to be in the study,
as noted in Tables 3 and 4.

Random assignment of mediation participants into experimental and
control groups was ruled out because of ethical issues and concerns of
program staff. The initial design for the study included the use of systematic random samples at all sites. It became evident early in the study that
this would simply not be possible, primarily because of the relatively
limited number of cases referred by the court to each of the three primary
program sites, the number of cases that eventually reached mediation and
the difficulty of contacting individuals following the mediation. The desired
sample size for analysis purposes would not have been achieved. An
availability sample was therefore used for both the experimental and
comparison group samples.

Non-Participating Referrals

Victims and offenders who were referred to the mediation process by
the courts during the same time period, but who did not participate, served
as one of the two comparison groups in this study. Particularly since these
individuals had already indicated their lack of interest in being involved
in the program, it was expected that they would have a limited interest in
being interviewed for the study. The "referred-but-no-mediation" sample
of 198 victims and offenders (see Table 2), across all sites, represented
approximately 5% of the total number of victims and offenders in cases
referred to but not entering mediation during 1990 and 1991.

NOT-REFERRED-TO-MEDIATION SAMPLE

The second comparison group, drawn from the same jurisdictions, consisted of an availability sample of similar offenders and their victims who were not referred to the mediation process. These offenders were matched on the variables of age, sex, race and offense with those offenders in the mediation sample. The "non-referral-to-mediation" sample of 218 (see Table 2), across all sites, represented approximately 10% of the total cases mediated during 1990 and 1991.

Table 2: Samples for Individuals Interviewed

	REFERRED TO MEDIATION		NOT REFERRED TO MEDIATION (COMPARISON GROUP #2)	TOTAL
	PARTICIPATING	NON-PARTICIPATING (COMPARISON GROUP #1)		
ALBUQUERQUE				
-victims	73	33	25	131
-offenders	65	36	28	129
MINNEAPOLIS				
-victims	96	51	72	219
-offenders	81	40	71	192
OAKLAND				
-victims	61	19	10	90
-offenders	56	19	12	87
AUSTIN				
-victims	50		50	
-offenders	50		50	
TOTAL	532	198	218	948

Most of the victims and offenders who participated in mediation were interviewed before and after the mediation, resulting in a total of 1,153 interviews.

Victims and offenders in both of the comparison groups participated in one interview that was similar to the post-mediation interview. The sub-samples for the mediation group and the two comparison groups are described in Tables 2, 3 and 4.

Table 3: Characteristics of Victim Samples

COMBINED SITES	MEDIATION PARTICIPANTS	REFERRED BUT NO MEDIATION	NON-REFERRAL TO MEDIATION
Age:			
a. mean	35	33	36
b. range	7-89	7-71	8-79
Gender:			
a. female	45%	41%	40%
b. male	55%	59%	60%
Ethnicity:			
a. Asian	2%	3%	2%
b. Black	5%	9%	2%
c. Caucasian (Anglo)	74%	69%	87%
d. Caucasian (Hispanic)	16%	13%	8%
e. Other	3%	6%	1%
Highest Grade of Education:			
a. 8th	10%	12%	unavailable
b 9th	2%	7%	
c. 10th	2%	5%	
d. 11th	6%	6%	
e. 12th	27%	30%	
f. Assoc/dgr	24%	20%	
g. College/Bach	20%	13%	
h. Graduate/dgr	9%	7%	

It should be noted that only a subset of the mediation participants in Hennepin County, MN (post-adjudication cases), representing the largest site, was selected for generating the matched sample of non-referral-to-mediation offenders. This explains why the characteristics of the mediation and the non-referral-to-mediation samples above are not identical.

Table 4: Characteristics of Offender Samples

COMBINED SITES	MEDIATION	REFERRED BUT NO MEDIATION	NON-REFERRAL TO MEDIATION
Age:			
a. mean	15	13	16
b. range	8-18	10-18	9-18
Gender:			
a. female	13%	12%	5%
b. male	87%	88%	95%
Ethnicity:			
a. Amer.Indian	3%	3%	1%
b. Asian	2%	4%	1%
c. Black	17%	14%	6%
d. Caucasian (Anglo)	51%	49%	72%
e. Caucasian (Hispanic)	26%	29%	18%
f. Other	1%	1%	2%
Highest Grade of Education:			
a. 5th	6%	31%	unavailable
b. 6th	11%	13%	
c. 7th	8%	20%	
d. 8th	16%	20%	
e. 9th	15%	15%	
f. 10th	21%	1%	
g. 11th	16%		
e. 12th	7%		
Prior offenses:			
a. yes	27%	34%	12%
b. no	73%	66%	88%
Referral point:			
a. diversion	59%	40%	54%
b. post-adjud.	21%	32%	15%
c. post-dispo.	20%	28%	32%

DATA COLLECTION INSTRUMENTS

Fourteen data collection instruments developed especially for the study were employed. The interview schedules consisted of both open-ended and closed-ended items, including Likert-type questions. No relevant pre-existing instruments were available, other than those that had been developed by the principal investigator and the senior research associate during prior studies (Coates and Gehm, 1989; Umbreit, 1991c). Precisely because the primary instruments in this study were based upon an enhanced version of prior instruments developed and applied by project staff at multiple sites, and because no significant differences were found in applying the new instruments at multiple sites, a strong degree of reliability was present. The construct validity of the instruments was strengthened through their development in collaboration with a panel of practitioners. Triangulation of data sources contributed to convergent validity. Taken together, the 14 instruments allowed for cross-validation of both qualitative and quantitative data sources. Confidence in the validity of findings was strengthened where similar findings emerged from different data sources. The instruments consisted of:

(1) Pre-mediation victim interview schedule

(2) Post-mediation victim interview schedule

(3) Pre-mediation offender interview schedule

(4) Post-mediation offender interview schedule

(5) Referred/no-mediation victim interview schedule

(6) Referred/no-mediation offender interview schedule

(7) Non-referral victim interview schedule

(8) Non-referral offender interview schedule

(9) Program staff interview schedule

(10) Court official interview schedule

(11) Mediation observation protocols

(12) Coding form for restitution completion record data

(13) Coding form for recidivism record data

(14) Coding form for cost-analysis record data

The data collection instruments were pre-tested with a small sample of participants at each site.

Interview Data

1. Interview Schedule for Victims and Offenders in Mediation

A standardized interview schedule, consisting of closed-ended (including Likert scales) and open-ended questions with probes, was administered before and after mediation. Both the pre- and post-mediation schedules focused on the impact of mediation, client satisfaction, and the participant's understanding of justice and attitudes toward the courts. The pre-mediation schedule contained fewer open-ended questions with probes, and was designed to be administered in a brief phone interview within a week prior to the mediation. The post-mediation schedule contained more open-ended questions with probes, and was designed to be administered in person approximately two months after the mediation.

2. Comparison Groups

A standardized interview schedule, consisting of closed-ended (including Likert scales) and open-ended questions with probes, was administered to the two comparison groups (referred/no-mediation group and non-referral-to-mediation group) approximately two months after the disposition date for the case. The interview schedule focused on the impact of mediation, client satisfaction, and the participant's understanding of justice and attitudes toward the courts. It contained fewer open-ended questions with probes than the post-mediation interviews schedules, and was designed to be administered in a brief phone interview.

3. Interview Schedule for Program Staff

A structured interview schedule, consisting primarily of open-ended questions, was administered to the program director at each site. Questions focused upon the initial development of the program, changes that have occurred over time and plans for the future. Various characteristics of the program, its funding sources and case management procedures were also addressed.

4. Interview Schedule for Court Officials

A structured interview schedule, consisting of both open-ended and closed-ended questions, was administered to a sample of judges, probation staff and any other relevant court officials that have in one way or another been affected by the victim-offender mediation program.

Observation Data

5. Observation Protocols

As this study examined the impact of the victim-offender mediation process on participants, it was important to observe a sample of actual mediation sessions at each of the program sites. Observation protocols were developed in order to capture a systematic picture of how the mediation process occurred. Particular emphasis was placed on how the mediator moved from the initial introduction, to encouraging the sharing of feelings related to the conflict, to negotiation of restitution and final resolution. The observation protocols were pre-tested with several cases in Minnesota.

Record Data

6. Coding Form for Restitution Completion

Data related to completion of restitution obligations by offenders were obtained from both program records and court records. A coding form was developed to systematically collect and record this data.

7. Coding Form for Recidivism Data

A coding form was used to systematically collect and record data in court records related to subsequent charges and adjudications. The type and degree of subsequent delinquent behavior was identified in order to determine its relative severity to prior delinquent behavior.

8. Coding Form for Cost Analysis

In order to examine potential cost implications to the court that are related to the operation of victim-offender mediation programs, a coding form was developed to record all relevant cost items so that a unit cost of mediation services could then be determined.

Pre-test: Reliability and Validity Check

The data collection instruments were pre-tested with a small sample of participants at each site. Because of likely regional—if not cultural—differences between the program sites, it was important to assess whether the questions in the instruments had the same meaning at all sites. Having four different persons conduct the pre-test interviews provided a good reliability check. As a validity check, the specific wording of questions in the interview schedule, including those related to the Likert-type questions, was examined during the pre-test of the instrument.

Safeguards for Human Subjects

Research subjects were informed of the purpose of the study and their right to refuse to participate. A "consent-to-participate" form and telephone protocol was developed for all research subjects. The names of all research subjects were filed in a locked cabinet, separately from the data, with a number code available for appropriate data retrieval. All names were destroyed at the end of the project. Findings are presented in aggregate form; names of specific individual victims and offenders do not appear in the final report, with the exception of key program staff or court officials who gave permission to use their name.

Qualitative Data Analysis

Data analysis related to the face-to-face interviews began during the data collection phase. More intense analysis, which occurred after the completion of all the interviews, consisted of three essential components: data reduction, data display and conclusion drawing/verification (Miles and Huberman, 1984). Data reduction consisted of focusing and simplifying the qualitative data emerging from the interviews. Coding of data was important during this process. Data display consisted of organizing and presenting the data in a format that facilitated conclusion drawing and verification. This required organizing and presenting the data under the specific themes that were emerging.

Conclusion drawing was based upon the emergence of regularities, patterns and explanations. The meanings emerging from the data were then verified and tested for their plausibility and confirmability (i.e., validity). Cross-validation (data triangulation) of qualitative and quantitative data was employed in the verification process. As Denzin (1978) and Patton (1980) note, triangulation represents a mixing of methodologies to allow the researcher to be more confident in the findings. Data triangulation, specifically, involved the use of two or more data sources in a study.

Validity Check: Data Triangulation

A major strength of qualitative data lies in the validity of observations that are made in a more natural setting, and that provide more in-depth and contextual material. Yet, multiple data sources often can provide more valid conclusions. Data that emerged from the open-ended interview questions were cross-validated with the quantitative data provided by the Likert scales. This required examining the large volume of data from the open-ended questions and then cross-validating it with responses to identical questions in the form of Likert scales.

Quantitative Data Analysis

A major portion of the quantitative analysis was descriptive, depicting background characteristics of participants, level of satisfaction, and outcomes related to restitution and recidivism. This included frequencies and percentages. Quantitative analysis also focused upon examining whether any significant differences existed within the four program sites between mediation participants, those who were referred but did not mediate and those not referred to mediation. The differences across sites were also explored to determine if size of program, length of program experience or characteristics of participants were related to differential impact.

Since the level of measurement represented nominal and ordinal data, chi-square was employed as the appropriate non-parametric test. For analysis purposes, the five-point Likert scales were converted to a dichotomous variable. The criterion for a finding of significance was .05.

STRENGTHS AND LIMITATIONS OF STUDY

This multi-site analysis of victim-offender mediation is the largest study of its kind in the U.S. It was more rigorous than previous research because of a number of factors.

Client satisfaction and perceptions of fairness were examined through the use of pre- and post-mediation instruments. Post-mediation data were analyzed through the use of two comparison groups: (1) victims and offenders who were referred to the mediation program but did not participate in mediation ("referred/no mediation"); and (2) victims and offenders from the same jurisdiction who have been matched (with the mediation sample) along the variables of age, race, sex, and prior offenses but who were never referred to the mediation program ("non-referral").

This study represents the first attempt to examine the impact of mediation on the successful completion of restitution. As noted earlier, restitution completion by offenders in victim-offender mediation programs was analyzed though the use of a comparison group from the same jurisdiction that was matched along the variables of age, race, sex, offense and restitution amount. Offenders in this matched sample were ordered to pay restitution through the existing restitution program in the probation office.

The actual process of mediation, including mediator styles, was examined through observations of mediation sessions. Through the use of an observation protocol and a mediator assessment instrument, the process of mediating conflict between crime victims and their offenders could be more thoroughly analyzed.

No other study has examined the cost implications of operating victim-offender mediation programs in a number of different jurisdictions in the U.S. Cost data related to the development and operation of mediation programs in several cites, including the unit cost per referral or per mediation, were collected and analyzed.

There were, however, a number of limitations in this cross-site analysis of victim-offender mediation. The findings that have emerged cannot be generalized to other victim-offender mediation programs that were not in the study. Because a true experimental design, with random assignment of subjects to an experimental and control group, was not possible, the conclusions and implications offered are at best suggestive.

The lack of available relevant instruments in this new field of victim-offender mediation, with well-tested and high degrees of validity and reliability, required that entirely new instruments of a survey nature be developed. While they were tested for reasonable levels of validity and reliability, these instruments may lack the strength that comes with pre-existing and well-tested instruments.

The level of measurement employed in the instruments was either nominal or ordinal. Even the Likert-type questions were collapsed into dichotomous variables for the purposes of analysis. Therefore, the vast majority of data represent nominal data. The absence of true interval data required that only non-parametric tests be employed. As such, the chi-square test for two independent samples was employed most frequently, with a criterion of .05 for significance.

The pre- and post-mediation measurement, as mentioned above, was part of the strength of the design of this study. As the instruments were administered, however, it became clear that the "pre" measurement occurred too late in the process. By the time the pre-mediation interview was conducted—after the mediator had secured the interest of the party—a good portion of the overall mediation intervention had occurred. The victim or offender had been listened to, received information about the program and expressed a commitment to participate. Their expectations were fairly high. This probably explained the frequent lack of significant change between the pre- and post-mediation interviews, when analyzed by individual rather than group. Efforts to conduct the pre-mediation interview prior to having any contact with the mediation staff were considered, but no acceptable procedure could be determined by research and program staff that would not interfere with the required case management procedures.

Despite these limitations, however, it was the belief of the author that the strengths of this multi-site study of victim-offender mediation far outweighed whatever limitations were present. It will be important to address these limitations in future research, including the need for a longitudinal study to examine possible long-term effects of the mediation process.

4. Program Sites and Participants

- *Three of the programs were operated by private non-profit agencies in Albuquerque, Minneapolis and Oakland.*
- *One of the programs was operated by a juvenile probation office in Austin.*
- *Victims' primary expectation was to both recover their loss and help the offender.*
- *Offenders' primary expectation was to "make things right."*
- *91% of victims indicated voluntary participation.*
- *81% of offenders indicated voluntary participation.*
- *Victims who chose not to participate in mediation indicated the following reasons: lack of time; settlement was reached before mediation; and no desire to meet offender because they were too angry.*

Victim-offender mediation programs in four states participated in the study. The program in Albuquerque serves an urban jurisdiction with large Hispanic and Native-American communities. The program in Minneapolis serves both Hennepin County (Minneapolis area) and Ramsey County (St. Paul area), although by far the largest number of cases are referred by the juvenile court in Hennepin County. The program in Oakland serves the wider East Bay area, with most referrals being received from communities outside Oakland itself. All of the research questions were examined at these sites.

The fourth site, in Austin, was added later in the study since it offered an interesting variable to examine. Whereas the three primary programs were all operated by private, non-profit agencies (reflecting the majority of victim offender mediation programs in the U.S.), the program in Austin was sponsored by the local juvenile probation office. A far more limited range of data collection and analysis occurred at the Austin program site.

The four program sites were selected for a variety of reasons. Each was at a point of development in which there existed a relatively stable stream of case referrals from the court and/or probation. A good deal of regional and programmatic diversity was found in these four sites. Finally, all of the sites expressed interest in participating in the study and were willing to commit the resources of their agency over time.

Each of the four program sites will be described below. Important characteristics of the programs, including developmental issues, will be highlighted. First, the three primary sites will be presented. Then, the fourth site in Austin, which entered the study at a later point, will be addressed.

It should be noted that a "case" is defined as each victim-offender combination. Therefore, a crime involving one offender and three victims would be counted as three cases since a good deal of work has to be done with each separate victim unit.

ALBUQUERQUE PROGRAM

The Victim Offender Mediation Program (VOMP) in Albuquerque is a rather unique joint public- and private-sector venture. While most other victim-offender mediation programs throughout the country that are operated by private, non-profit agencies work closely with the local courts and particularly probation officials, the Albuquerque model appears to be one of the first to be designed as a jointly administered and funded program. The program is jointly sponsored and administered by the New Mexico Center for Dispute Resolution and the Juvenile Probation Office of the New Mexico Youth Authority. It began in the fall of 1987 and currently has an annual caseload of nearly 400 referrals.

The New Mexico Center for Dispute Resolution is a private, non-profit, community-based agency established in 1982 that provides a range of mediation and conflict-resolution services. In fact, the New Mexico Center for Dispute Resolution is one of the more comprehensive mediation programs in the country that sponsors a victim-offender mediation program, particularly since it also operates a number of other youth-related mediation programs. These include: parent-child mediation with status offenders referred by the courts in several local jurisdictions; school mediation; mediation training for youths in correctional institutions; and conflict resolution for violent juvenile offenders. In addition, the center provides training in conflict management that is tailored to specific organizations, such as health professionals.

The VOMP program in Albuquerque was originally designed to receive referrals from both the district attorney's office (diversion cases) and juvenile court judges (post-adjudication cases). During the first years of the program, most referrals involved non-violent property offenses, committed mainly by first offenders, that would be diverted from further penetration into the court system if mediation was successful in resolving the conflict, including the securing of restitution by the victim. Youths on probation were also referred. More recently, there has been an increase in cases that are referred at a post-adjudication level by the juvenile court.

The offices of the VOMP are located at the juvenile justice center, which provides quick access to all probation staff and clients as well as valuable "in-kind" support through free rent and supplies. In addition, VOMP staff become familiar to other probation staff rather than being seen as "outsiders." While sharing office space and entering the culture of probation staff is clearly beneficial to the program, it also requires VOMP staff to simultaneously maintain their own separate identity. They are mediators, not probation officers. A certain healthy tension needs to be present, and this reality is openly affirmed by Albuquerque's Chief Probation Officer Doug Mitchell.

The juvenile probation office has designated one of their staff to serve as the restitution director. Part of this person's responsibility is to assist with the intake process by identifying appropriate cases to refer to the mediation program, and to monitor the payment of restitution.

Once a case is referred, VOMP staff or volunteer mediators call and meet with the offender and victim separately, if both agree to do so. During these separate meetings, the mediator listens to their story, explains the mediation program, encourages their participation and, if they choose to enter mediation, schedules a mediation session.

The New Mexico Center for Dispute Resolution is responsible for recruiting, training and coordinating all volunteer mediators. Together with the juvenile probation office, the center is also responsible for securing funds and building public support for victim-offender mediation. During the early life of the project, there was some difficulty in working out the boundaries of this public/private-sector partnership. What initially began as a potential obstacle, however, later turned out to be a major strength of this collaborative effort. VOMP staff are now recognized as fostering a culture of mediation within the entire probation office, with potential benefits well beyond the victim-offender mediation program itself. Rather than being co-opted by the larger bureaucracy, the presence of VOMP staff, on a daily basis, has made a positive contribution to the larger organizational culture by promoting the values of direct communication and conflict resolution.

From the beginning of the program in Albuquerque, volunteer mediators were extensively used. Use of volunteers was important in that it encouraged community participation in the program, and also represented a cost-effective way of administering the program. A total of 16 hours of training, conducted by a consultant, was initially provided to each volunteer prior to handling a case alone. The training focused upon the victim and offender experience, the mediation process and role plays to practice mediation skills. Mediators are now required to complete a total of 40 hours of training, with additional time spent on skill-building exercises related to communication and conflict resolution. Training is provided by staff of the New Mexico Center for Dispute Resolution, and nearly all cases are handled by co-mediators.

While the VOMP in Albuquerque remains committed to using volunteer mediators, it has become increasingly aware of the investment of time and energy in recruiting, training, coordinating and nurturing volunteers. Managing a large number of people with different personalities and schedules can, at times, be quite difficult and time consuming. The benefits of using trained volunteers, however, continue to be far greater than the cost.

During the initial development of the VOMP in Albuquerque, the support of the juvenile court judge and the chief probation officer was absolutely critical. While both of these individuals provided overall support, it was the restitution director in the probation department who played an active, day-to-day role in developing and administering the program.

As the VOMP developed over the years, the support of the juvenile court judges has remained vital to the continuing development of the program. Probation staff, however, remain the most actively involved on a daily basis with the administration of the VOMP. The support of the chief juvenile probation officer remains crucial to the growth and development of the program.

The most critical issue related to the development of the Victim Offender Mediation Program in Albuquerque has clearly been securing the financial resources to initially begin and then continue operation of the program. During the early months, the New Mexico Center for Dispute Resolution had only limited designated funding for the VOMP. In addition to relatively small grants from the state victim agency and the city and county governments, the center also used some of its general support funds to cover a portion of the cost of staff time. In 1990, the VOMP was able to secure a State Youth Authority grant to further develop and expand. Without the in-kind support (staff time and supplies) provided by the juvenile probation department, however, the VOMP would not have survived much beyond its first year. Ongoing state funding has now been secured. The other critical issue that the VOMP faced was the need to significantly refine its case management procedures, as noted above, so that the much larger number of case referrals could be efficiently processed.

More information about this program can be obtained through contacting:

Victim Offender Mediation Program

New Mexico Center for Dispute Resolution

620 Roma N.W. Albuquerque, NM 87102

(505) 247-0571

MINNEAPOLIS PROGRAM

One of the more well-developed programs in the U.S. is the Center for Victim Offender Mediation (CVOM) in Minneapolis. A program of the Citizens Council Mediation Services, the CVOM is sponsored by the Minnesota Citizens Council on Crime and Justice.

The CVOM began in 1985 and receives referrals of juvenile offenders from court services staff in Hennepin County (Minneapolis area) and Ramsey County (St. Paul area). The support of juvenile court judges and court services staff in both counties has played a vital role in both the early development of the program and its continued growth.

Once a case is referred by the court to the CVOM, it is assigned to a staff or volunteer mediator. Mediators are provided with approximately 25 hours of initial training, followed by periodic additional in-service training. During the early years of the program, however, only 12 hours of initial training was provided. The mediator first meets with the offender and victim separately to hear their story, explain the program and encourage participation. Participation in the mediation process is meant to be voluntary. If both agree, a mediation session is scheduled. The program in Minneapolis has done a particularly good job of presenting mediation as a truly voluntary option for offenders.

The program in Minneapolis was initially called VORP (Victim Offender Reconciliation Program). Before the program began in 1985, an extensive amount of technical assistance and training was provided over a two-year period by an out-of-state consultant, made available through the National

Institute of Corrections of the U.S. Department of Justice. This technical assistance proved to be quite helpful in determining the most appropriate program design, case management procedures and likely funding sources.

The program was designed to accept referrals of juvenile burglary cases only after a plea of guilty had been accepted by the court but prior to the disposition hearing. The offense of burglary was targeted because it represented a very serious and high-volume offense in which victims frequently experienced a great deal of emotional trauma as well as material loss. Rather than focusing on low-end cases that could trivialize the potential benefits of mediation, it was believed that the new program could have the greatest impact on both parties by targeting the more serious offense of residential burglary, a crime that was of major concern to the community at the time.

It was believed that this post-adjudication and pre-disposition point of referral was most appropriate for several reasons. Victims of crime could have direct input into part of the penalty that the court would require of their offender. Such direct and active involvement of victims in the justice system is rare. The offender's clear admission of guilt was present, and there would seem to be few, if any, of the due-process issues that are present in diversion cases (i.e., admitting one's guilt without the full benefit of due-process protections offered by the court, particularly if the mediation is unsuccessful). Offenders would likely have a good deal of motivation to participate in "making things right" prior to the disposition hearing. Also, judges would likely be more receptive to approving probation recommendations that included victim-offender mediation if, at the time of sentencing, they knew that the victim and offender had already met and agreed to the restitution plan that was attached to the pre-disposition report before the judge.

In Hennepin County, approximately 30 days elapsed between the acceptance of a plea of guilty and the disposition hearing. The case would be referred by either probation staff or restitution program staff within a week or so of the court acceptance of the guilty plea. The victim-offender mediation program would then need to call the parties, meet with them separately and conduct the mediation. They would need to get the signed restitution agreement back to the probation or restitution staff in time for them to include it in their disposition report to the court. Unfortunately, this 30-day "window" proved to be too small. In practice, the window was reduced to only two or three weeks.

During the initial year of the program, only a small number of cases were referred. By limiting referrals to burglary only, the program was clearly being underutilized. Moreover, handling cases (contacting the parties, making arrangements and conducting the mediation) during the window between adjudication and disposition proved to be too difficult in a large urban area such as Hennepin County.

Referral and case management procedures were later changed to accept any property offenses or minor assaults at any point within the process. This could include cases that were diverted from prosecution, cases following adjudication but prior to the disposition hearing, or cases that were referred after the dispositional hearing. Even more important, the program negotiated and implemented far more assertive referral procedures in which program staff would frequently review potential cases at the probation office and select those that seemed appropriate. In Ramsey County, a mediation staff person was housed in a branch office of the juvenile probation department. This proved to be extremely helpful in building better rapport between the victim offender mediation program and probation staff, and, particularly, in receiving case referrals.

The CVOM is now one of several programs of the Citizens Council Mediation Services, sponsored by the Minnesota Citizens Council on Crime and Justice. Mediation Services also has a parent-child mediation program, a school mediation program and a youth in correctional institutions program. Staff members of Mediation Services are increasingly providing technical assistance and training for other mediation programs in the state of Minnesota. The Minnesota Citizens Council on Crime and Justice is a United Way agency with a long history—over 30 years—of providing services to offenders, crime victims, families of offenders and the general public, through educational materials and policy reports.

During its early years, the program in Minneapolis had only limited referrals and only marginal support from the larger juvenile justice system. Today, the program has one of the larger caseloads of any victim-offender mediation program in the U.S., enjoys strong support from judges and probation staff in both Hennepin and Ramsey counties, and has developed an increasingly strong funding base to support its work.

The most critical issues now facing the CVOM are continuing to institutionalize its funding base, and expanding its program to service adult offenders and their victims.

More information on this program can be obtained through contacting:

Citizens Council Mediation Services
Minnesota Citizens Council on Crime and Justice
822 South Third Street
Minneapolis, MN 55415
(612) 340-5432

OAKLAND PROGRAM

In October of 1986, Catholic Charities of Oakland began to explore the possible development of a new victim-offender reconciliation program to serve the East Bay area. The agency had a long history of working with the socially disadvantaged, including persons affected by the criminal justice system. In addition, the Catholic Charities of Oakland Diocese was involved in refugee and immigrant services, employment and placement services, counseling, services for seniors, and services for the physically and developmentally disabled.

Meetings were held with key juvenile justice system contacts, including various representatives of the juvenile court in Contra Costa County. An out-of-state consultant assisted local program staff as they designed the new program and attempted to secure public and system support for it. This consultant also provided the initial mediation training for volunteers. Particularly influential in the initial decision to work with a non-profit community agency like Catholic Charities was Juvenile Probation Director Thomas E. Jimison and Superior Court Judge John C. Minney. After reviewing various programs, collecting material, and talking with local court officials, Catholic Charities made a commitment in June of 1987 to establish a Victim Offender Reconciliation Program (VORP) for juvenile offenders.

The VORP was to be part of the Office of Prisoner and Community Justice at Catholic Charities in Oakland. This criminal justice ministry coordinated activities related to prisoner advocacy and visitation, education for both victims and offenders, and involvement in larger reform efforts in the Bay Area. Catholic Charities worked in both Alameda County (Oakland) and neighboring Contra Costa County to the east.

The program began with a budget of approximately $20,000 and a staff consisting of one full-time equivalent (FTE) employee working on a half-time schedule. By 1990 the budget had increased to $75,000 and a staff of three FTEs (one of whom is a VISTA-type volunteer who receives a stipend). The VORP was originally supported through general funds of the sponsoring agency (representing individual donors), and through a grant of $5,000 from a local foundation. During 1990, the program was funded by a $36,000 grant from Alameda County, an $11,350 grant from Contra Costa County and the balance from discretionary funds provided by Catholic Charities. Both of the county grants were made possible by fairly recent California law that provided funds for local dispute-resolution programs through a court filing fee and that were to be administered through local county committees.

The new VORP was designed to accept referral of juveniles offenders from the courts and probation offices in Contra Costa and Alameda counties. These youths had committed primarily property offenses. Actual case referrals could occur at either a diversion level or a post-adjudication level, although most cases were referred at the diversion level. Initially, most case referrals came from Contra Costa County. In the last couple of years this has changed dramatically, with most referrals now coming from Alameda County (outside the city of Oakland itself).

Cases would first be identified by the probation department based upon the following referral criteria: property offense; first or second offense; and identifiable loss requiring restitution. After the probation department referred the case to the VORP, program staff would then send a letter to both parties informing them that their case had been referred to the VORP and mentioning that mediators would be contacting them. The mediators would call the offender and then conduct an individual meeting with the offender and his or her parents. During this meeting, the mediator introduced the VORP process, listened to their story, collected information, and offered the offender and his or her parents the opportunity to participate in mediation if their victim was willing to do so. A brief call would then be made by a mediator to set up an individual meeting between the mediators and the victim. During the individual meeting with the victim, the mediators would introduce the VORP process, listen to the victim's story, assess the impact that the crime had upon the victim, collect information about actual losses and invite the victim's participation in the program.

It should be noted that, while participation by the offender clearly had a less than voluntary dimension because of referral from the court system, participation in mediation was not mandatory and the volunteer's role was to make that clear to the youth and his or her parents. Additionally, participation of the victim was meant to be entirely voluntary.

Following these two individual meetings—one with the offender and one with the victim—the actual face-to-face mediation session was scheduled and conducted. The mediation sessions began with an opening statement by the mediator to explain his or her role, present ground rules and identify the agenda for the meeting. The first part of the meeting was meant to focus upon what happened and how the parties felt about it. The second part was to focus upon the losses incurred by the victim and the need to negotiate a restitution agreement that was considered fair to both. Immediately after the opening statement by the mediator, both the offender and the victim would have some uninterrupted time to tell their stories.

The case management system employed by this program, as well as the vast majority of victim-offender mediation and reconciliation programs operated by private, non-profit agencies, is quite different from the process used by most community dispute resolution centers. Rather than having staff do the initial case development work, with mediators being totally removed and not entering the process until the time of the mediation session, mediators in the VORP handle the case from the initial contact with both parties through the mediation. This continuity in the mediator's role helps to build trust and increases a party's willingness to participate in mediation.

From its inception in 1988, the VORP of Catholic Charities in the East Bay area has used volunteer mediators. It was believed that direct community involvement in a program like the VORP was important, as well as the more practical recognition of needing to stretch their limited resources. During the early months of the program there were six community volunteers. Today there is a pool of about 80 volunteers. The program routinely uses comediators in all cases, and therefore a much larger pool of volunteers is required.

Training of volunteers has evolved with the program. Initially, volunteers received only 12 hours of training, which consisted of a basic overview of the program, case management steps, mediation techniques and role playing of mediations. Today volunteers receive an initial 30 hours of training consisting of all of the above elements of training, plus more extensive material on communication skills (active listening, effective speaking, balancing power, defusing anger, cross-cultural issues), teamwork, and an examination of their own assumptions about conflict and communication. The program also conducts continuing education events for volunteers and a training-for-trainers program where experienced volunteers develop their own training skills. The program views ongoing skill development as a payoff for volunteers' involvement, and a way to keep volunteers interested and excited about their work. The most critical issue that faces the program in Oakland is that of securing more stable ongoing funding to support its work.

More information about this program can be obtained through contacting:

Victim Offender Reconciliation Program

Catholic Charities

433 Jefferson Street Oakland, CA 94607

(510) 834-5656

AUSTIN PROGRAM

A fourth site in Austin, TX was added quite late in the study. This program began in early 1990 and is operated by the Travis County Probation Department, in conjunction with the Travis County Dispute Resolution Center. Precisely because all of the initial three sites are sponsored by private agencies, the Austin program offered a unique addition to the original design of the study, by allowing for analysis of any possible effects of a public-versus-private victim-offender mediation program upon client satisfaction and perceptions of fairness.

The Travis County Juvenile Court Department operates under the "balanced approach" philosophy, which requires a greater balance in responding to the needs of offenders, victims and the community. Juvenile offenders are held accountable for their behavior through the active involvement of victims in determining restitution. In addition, the offenders are offered a plan to build their individual competencies through creative community service, with the active involvement of community agencies and businesses. They are to be appropriately supervised for the purposes of protecting the public. Two court and probation units supervise approximately 500 juvenile offenders. They implement the balanced approach by providing stringent community-based supervision to protect the public (which may include electronic monitoring), and a case plan to address accountability and individual competency concerns.

Through the accountability component of the balanced approach, the Travis County Juvenile Court Department attempts to instill in youths a sense of owning their criminal behavior and facing the consequences of it. It is here that the victim-offender mediation program fits into the balanced approach, along with monetary restitution to the victim and community service restitution. The accountability as well as the competency-building components of the program are guided by the Program Support Unit in the juvenile court department.

The victim-offender mediation services are provided by the Travis County Juvenile Court Department in cooperation with the Travis County Dispute Resolution Center, which provides a wide range of mediation and conflict-resolution services in the community. The juvenile court develops the case by contacting and preparing youths and their victims for the mediation process. Case development includes assisting victims in documenting monetary loss, applying for state funds under the Victim's Compensation Act and furnishing victims with any needed referral information.

After the initial case development, the case is then scheduled for one of two evenings during the week during which a mediator from the Travis County Dispute Resolution Center will be available. The mediation case developer from the juvenile court is present during the evening of the mediation, and briefs the mediator prior to the session. This procedure—in which the mediator has no prior contact with the victim and offender through the period of case development—is different from those used in the vast majority of other victim-offender mediation programs throughout the U.S., including the three primary program sites in this study. The procedure is, however, quite consistent with how many mediation programs handle neighborhood disputes.

The program aims to promote offender accountability and build competency through the juvenile's participation in conflict resolution sessions. For the victims, the desired outcomes for this process include restoring the victim's loss and addressing any of their continuing concerns resulting from the crime. Mediation case developers manage their own caseloads, as well as serve as a resource to all probation officers regarding victim/offender restitution.

More information about this program can be obtained through contacting:

Victim Offender Mediation Program

Travis County Juvenile Court

2515 South Congress Avenue

Austin, TX 78704

(512) 448-7000

Table 5: 1991 Program Characteristics

CHARACTERISTIC	ALBU-QUER-QUE	AUSTIN	MINNEA-POLIS	OAKLAND
Start date	1987	1990	1985	1987
Primary referral source	probation	probation	probation	probation
Sponsorship/ management	private	public	private	private
Total 1991 budget	$31,530	$106,241	$123,366	$127,176
Number of staff	1.5 FTE	3.5 FTE	3.6 FTE	3.5 FTE
Use of co-mediators	always	always	sometimes	always
Number of volunteer mediators	32	NA	30	80
Length of mediation training	40 hrs	40 hrs	25 hrs	30 hrs
Total 1991 case referrals	391	853	453	368
Total mediations in 1991	108	246	179	129
Proportion of mediations to case referrals in 1991	28%	29%	40%	35%

CHARACTERISTICS OF REFERRALS

Table 6 indicates the characteristics of offenders at the four program sites.

Taken together, two of three cases referred to the four programs occurred prior to formal adjudication, as a diversion effort. As Table 7 indicates, the remaining cases (31%) were referred following formal adjudication by the juvenile court. While the proportion of post-adjudication referrals at individual sites varied from 2% in Austin to 41% in Minneapolis, the vast majority of cases at all sites represented pre-adjudication referrals.

Table 6: Offender Characteristics (1990-91)

VARIABLE	ALBU-QUER-QUE	AUSTIN	MINNEA-POLIS	OAK-LAND	TOTAL
1. Average offender age	15	15	15	15	15
2. Offender age range	10-19	10-17	10-18	7-18	7-18
3. Offender gender					
a. Male	90%	87%	82%	82%	86%
b. Female	10%	13%	18%	18%	14%
4.Offender race					
a. Caucasian	30%	31%	70%	64%	54%
b. Black	2%	25%	23%	15%	14%
c. Hispanic	65%	42%	2%	15%	27%
d. Other Minorities	3%	2%	5%	6%	5%

Table 7: Referral Characteristics (1990-91)

VARIABLE	ALBU-QUER-QUE	AUSTIN	MINNEA-POLIS	OAK-LAND	TOTAL
1. Cases referred	591	1,107	450	173	823
2. Pre-adjudication	76%	98%	59%	88%	69%
3 Post-adjudication	24%	2%	41%	12%	31%
4. Individual victims	593	1,058	317	115	634
5. Individual offenders	604	1,087	332	111	656
6. Type of offenses					
a. Against property	73%	81%	89%	84%	87%
b. Against people	27%	19%	11%	16%	13%
Most frequent property offense	burglary	burglary	vanda-lism	vanda-lism	vanda-lism
Most frequent violent offense	assault	assault	assault	assault	assault

CLIENT EXPECTATIONS FOR MEDIATION

Victims and offenders who participated in a mediation session had a number of different expectations of the session. Victims were most likely to indicate that recovering their loss and helping the offender were equally the most important expectations they had. This was followed in frequency by the opportunity to tell the offender the effect of the crime and, finally, getting answers to questions they had about the crime. While only one in four victims indicated that they were nervous about the pending mediation session with their offender, nine of ten victims believed that the mediation session would probably be helpful.

Offenders were most likely to indicate that "making things right" was their primary expectation. This was followed in frequency by having the opportunity to apologize to the victim and, finally, being able "to be done with it." Only one of ten offenders indicated that they expected the mediation session with their victim to be less punishment than they would have otherwise received. Nearly half of the offenders, from the combined sites, stated that they were nervous about the pending mediation session with their victim. Six of ten offenders indicated that they cared about what the victim thought of them, and, similar to their victims, nine of ten offenders believed that the mediation session would be helpful.

VOLUNTARY PARTICIPATION IN MEDIATION

The question of whether victims and offenders actually participate voluntarily in mediation is crucial to the integrity of the mediation process. From the perspective of the young offender, it is important to have ownership in the mediation process and outcome. Moreover, if offenders are coerced into mediation against their will, this anger could be reflected in their behavior in the meeting with their victim.

A major concern of the victim rights movement is the issue of choice— allowing victims various options to regain a sense of power and control in their lives. If the mediation process is imposed upon victims of crime in a coercive manner, the experience itself could be victimizing.

While a high proportion of both victims (91%) and offenders (81%) clearly felt that their participation in mediation was voluntary, victims of crime were even more likely to indicate their belief that they were not coerced into mediation. For victims, there were no significant differences among the three program sites.

An earlier study by Coates and Gehm (1985) found that many offenders did not experience their involvement in mediation as voluntary. Particularly because of the highly coercive nature of any justice system's interaction with the offender, one would expect that many offenders in mediation would feel coerced into it. Yet, eight of ten offenders from the combined sites experienced their involvement in mediation as voluntary. There was, however, a significant difference found between program sites. The Minneapolis program had the highest rating of voluntary participation for offenders (90%), while the Albuquerque site had the lowest rating (71%).

REASONS FOR NON-PARTICIPATION IN MEDIATION

For those victims who were referred to a victim-offender mediation program, but chose not to participate, there were three major themes. The first theme focused upon the inconvenience of the mediation relative to the actual loss. This is reflected in such statements as "I didn't really have the time," and "the loss was small...it just wasn't worth the trouble." A second theme related to the fact that a number of victims had already directly worked out a settlement with the offender. In these cases, mediation was obviously not necessary. The third theme centered on the victim being too angry to meet the offender and/or disbelieving the offender's sincerity. "I really didn't want to see his face again; he would have just laughed." "I didn't want to see him because I would get mad." "This kid is so terrible and mean...flipping me off...I didn't want to ever see this jerk."

Offenders were far less clear in articulating the reasons they chose not to participate in mediation. The most frequent reasons focused upon their fear of facing the victim and their belief that doing so would not resolve anything. "I just didn't think that being brought together with her could solve anything."

More extensive data related to the reasons for non-participation in mediation was obtained at the Minneapolis program site. Table 8 identifies the reasons given by the 302 cases that were referred during 1991 but that did not enter mediation.

Table 8: Reasons for Non-Participation in Mediation, Minneapolis Program Site—1991

REASON	N	%
Victim unwilling to meet	64	21%
Offender unwilling to meet	17	6%
Couldn't find victim	18	6%
Couldn't find offender	19	6%
Situation already resolved	100	33%
Restitution agreement was mediated indirectly with no direct V/O contact	70	23%
Other	14	5%
TOTAL	302	100%

5. Immediate Outcomes of Mediation

- *A total of 1,131 mediations were held at the four programs during 1990-91.*
- *There was a 95% rate of successfully negotiating restitution agreements.*
- *Mediation had a significant effect on reducing victim's anxiety and sense of vulnerability.*
- *The opportunity for the victim to tell the offender the effect of the crime, get answers and negotiate restitution were the most important issues to victims.*
- *Actually receiving restitution was the least important issue to victims of juvenile crime.*
- *For offenders, telling the victim what happened, apologizing, negotiating and paying restitution were equally important issues.*

The victim-offender mediation process results in a number of different outcomes for both parties. In this chapter, immediate outcomes—such as the number of mediations held and the type and frequency of restitution agreements negotiated—will be presented. First, data will be presented for calendar year 1990 and 1991 separately. Then data will be presented for the combined two-year period representing calendar years 1990 and 1991. The chapters that follow will address the quality of justice outcomes (client satisfaction and perceptions of fairness), and mid-range outcomes (restitution completion and recidivism 12 months after the mediation).

The first outcome to be examined is that of mediation itself. In other words, of those cases referred to the victim-offender mediation program, how many actually result in a face-to-face mediation session? It is important to begin at this point since other potential material, emotional or informational benefits of mediation cannot occur unless the parties actually meet. It is frequently mentioned in the broader field of victim-offender mediation that approximately 50 to 60% of referred cases end up in a mediation session. We will report on a far broader range of "getting-them-to-the-table" rates, based on a two-year period at four program sites in different geographical regions of the U.S.

As can be seen in Figure 5, the proportion of referrals to victim-offender mediation that resulted in a mediation session ranged from a rate of 21% in Austin during 1990 to 64% in Minneapolis during 1990. There was a smaller range during 1991, with a low of 28% in Albuquerque to a high of 40% in Minneapolis. For the combined two-year period, the range was from 27% in Albuquerque and Austin to 52% in Minnesota. The average rate for all four sites combined was 39% in 1990, 33% in 1991 and 36% for the combined two-year period.

Figure 5: Proportion of Referrals Resulting in a Mediation Session

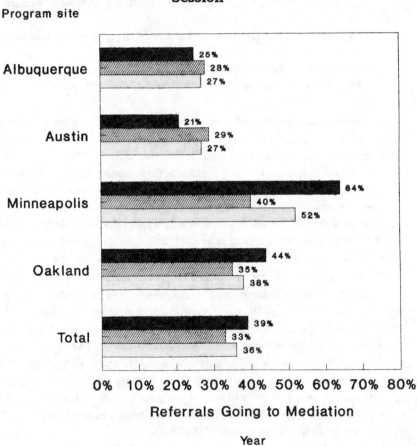

While the rates of referrals to mediation that result in a mediation session are lower in this study—with the exception of the Minneapolis site—a possible explanation may be found in the manner in which the referral process has changed over the years. In the early years of victim-offender mediation programs, including the three primary sites in this study, a list of criteria was provided to probation staff, and mediation program staff waited for cases to be referred. This relatively passive procedure resulted in fewer and much more selective cases being referred (i.e., those most likely to agree to mediation). In more recent years, all three primary research sites negotiated and implemented more assertive referral procedures. This resulted in mediation staff receiving a much larger number of cases. The proportion of this much larger number of cases that actually resulted in mediation, however, obviously decreased.

The average number of mediations held at the combined four program sites increased by 42% from 1990 (117 mediations) to 1991 (166 mediations). As Figure 6 indicates, during 1990 the number of mediations at individual program sites ranged from 50 in Albuquerque to 289 in Minneapolis. While the number of mediations increased during 1991— with the exception of the Minneapolis program site—the difference in the number of mediations across program sites was smaller, ranging from a low of 108 in Albuquerque to a high of 246 in Austin. The number of mediations in Minneapolis decreased 38% from 1990 to 1991. All other sites had large increases from 1990 to 1991 in the number of mediations held, ranging from a 70% increase in Oakland, a 116% increase in Albuquerque and a 192% increase in Austin.

The most obvious immediate outcome for those victims and offenders who chose to participate in mediation, as noted in Figure 7, is the highly probable successful negotiation of a restitution agreement, ranging from 90% in Oakland during 1991 to 99% in Albuquerque during 1991. For the combined two-year period of 1990 and 1991, the rate of successfully negotiated restitution agreements at the end of the mediation session for all four sites together was 95%. This represented a rate of 99% in Albuquerque, 98% in Austin, 93% in Minneapolis and 91% in Oakland.

These restitution agreements consisted of a variety of elements, as noted in Figure 8. Most (58%) focus upon payment of financial restitution by the offender to the victim. However, it was not unusual for agreements to include personal service for the victim (13%) or community service (29%), both of which are likely to result from conversion of a specific dollar amount of loss into hours of work, usually at an approximate minimum-wage rate. Some restitution agreements simply require an apology by the offender to their victim. At all of the four programs, financial restitution was clearly the main form of restitution that was negotiated and established during the mediation session between the victim and offender.

Figure 6: Number of Mediations Per Site

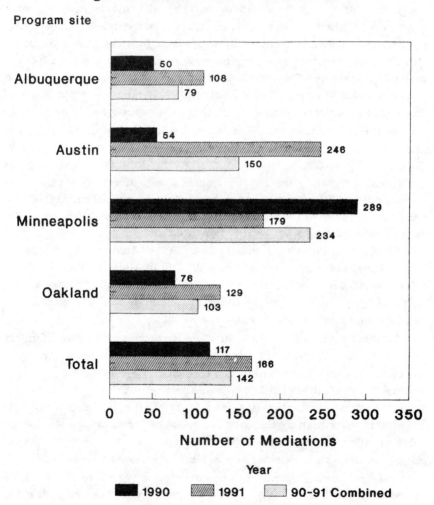

Program site

Albuquerque: 50 (1990), 108 (1991), 79 (90-91 Combined)
Austin: 54 (1990), 246 (1991), 150 (90-91 Combined)
Minneapolis: 289 (1990), 179 (1991), 234 (90-91 Combined)
Oakland: 76 (1990), 129 (1991), 103 (90-91 Combined)
Total: 117 (1990), 166 (1991), 142 (90-91 Combined)

Number of Mediations

Year

■ 1990   ▧ 1991   ▢ 90-91 Combined

Figure 7: Successfully Negotiated Restitution Agreements

Program site

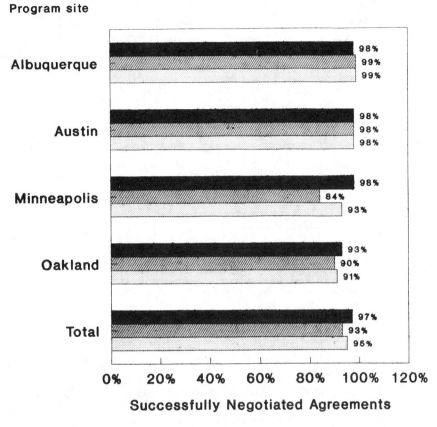

Figure 8: Frequency in Which Type of Restitution Appears in Agreements

Program site

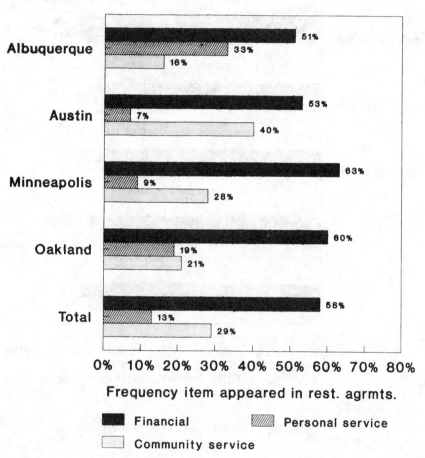

Frequency item appeared in rest. agrmts.

(Calendar Years 1990-91)

The average amount of financial restitution established in mediated agreements varied considerably at different program sites during 1990, ranging from $143 in Minneapolis to $457 in Albuquerque (see Figure 9). During 1991 there was a smaller difference between program sites, ranging from an average of $121 per agreement in Minneapolis to an average of $256 per agreement in Austin. For the combined two-year period of 1990 and 1991, the average amount of financial restitution per agreement across all program sides was $219.

Figure 9: Average Amount of Financial Restitution Per Negotiated Agreement

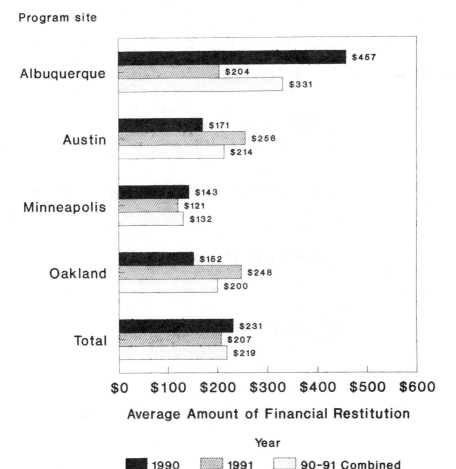

Program site

Average Amount of Financial Restitution

Year
1990   1991   90-91 Combined

As illustrated in Figure 10, the average number of personal service hours to be performed by the offender for the victim was in the range of 15 to 20 hours at all sites during both years, with the exception of Minneapolis in 1991, which had an average of only 7 hours of personal service for those restitution agreements that contained the element of personal service. Across all sites, the average was 21 hours of personal service during 1990, 16 hours during 1991 and 18 hours for the combined two-year period.

**Figure 10: Average Amount of Personal Service Restitution
Per Agreement**

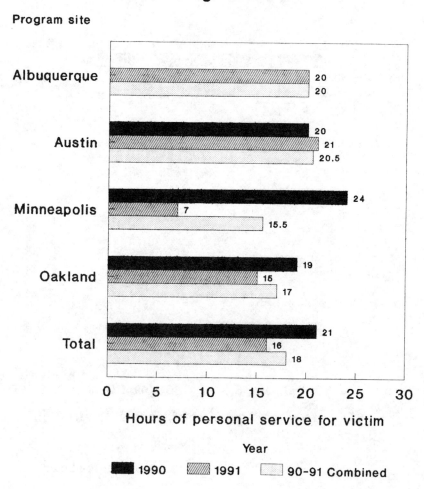

Community service represented the least frequent form of restitution to be included in the mediated agreements. During 1990, as noted in Figure 11, the average number of hours of community service per agreement ranged from 18 hours in Minneapolis to 29 hours in Albuquerque. During 1991, the range of community service hours across sites was a low of 10 hours in Oakland to a high of 44 hours in Albuquerque. For the combined two-year period of 1990 and 1991, the average number of community service hours per restitution agreement across all sites was 25 hours.

Figure 11: Average Amount of Community Service Restitution Per Agreement

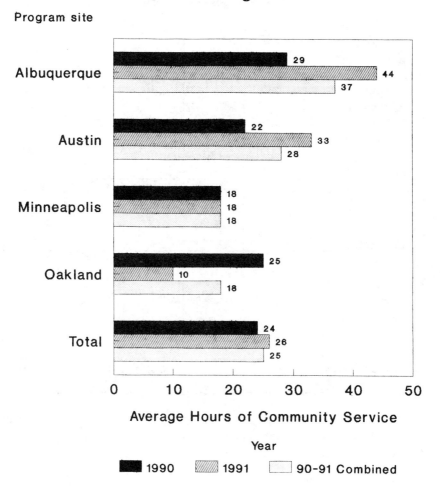

Table 9 provides a summary of the immediate outcomes that occurred across all four program sites during the combined two-year period of 1990 and 1991.

Table 9: Immediate Outcomes (1990-91)

VARIABLE	ALBU-QUERQUE	AUSTIN	MINNEA-POLIS	OAK-LAND	TOTAL
1. Number of mediations	158	300	468	205	1,131
2. Successfully negotiated restitution agreements	99%	98%	93%	91%	95%
3. Agreements with:					
a. Financial restitution	82	171	239	111	603
b. Personal service	57	21	31	36	145
c. Community service	29	130	107	39	305
4. Total financial restitution	$23,542	$41,536	$32,301	$23,227	$120,606
5. Average financial restitution	$287	$243	$135	$209	$200
6. Total personal service/hours	1,028	439	508	585	2,560
7. Average personal service	18 hrs	21 hrs	16 hrs	16 hrs	18 hrs
8. Total community service/hours	1,073	4,064	1,937	588	7,662
9. Average community service	37 hrs	31 hrs	18 hrs	15 hrs	25 hrs

Restitution contracts are not the only immediate outcome of the mediation program. And participants, after going through mediation, often indicate that other more important outcomes had occurred to them by

participation. Table 10 depicts two outcomes that underscore the importance of a face-to-face mediation. Crime victims from all of the sites
combined were significantly less upset about the crime and less fearful of
being revictimized by the same offender after they were able to meet him
or her in mediation. These findings held true at individual sites, with the
exception of Albuquerque (feeling upset about the crime) and Oakland
(afraid of being revictimized).

Table 10: Emotional Impact of Mediation on Victim

COMBINED SITES	PRE-MEDIATION % N	POST-MEDIATION % N	P VALUE
Upset about crime	67% (155)	49% (162)	p=.0001*
Afraid of being revictimized by offender	23% (154)	10% (166)	p=.003*

*Finding of significant difference

VICTIM/OFFENDER ATTITUDES ABOUT MEDIATION

Both victims and offenders identified a number of important issues
related to the process of talking about the crime and negotiating restitution. Negotiating restitution was important to nearly nine of ten victims at
both a pre- and post-mediation level. Actually receiving restitution, however, was important to only seven of ten victims. The opportunity to directly
participate in an interpersonal problem-solving process to establish a fair
restitution plan was more important to victims than actually receiving the
agreed-upon restitution.

As indicated in Table 11, significant differences were found between
pre- and post-mediation group samples related to the informational and
emotional needs of the victim, as well as the process of negotiating
restitution. Specifically, for victims to receive answers from the offender
about what happened, and to tell the offender how the crime affected them,
were both significantly more important after rather than before the actual
mediation session. This was also true of negotiating restitution with the

offender during the mediation session, even though actually receiving restitution was less important.

Table 11: Victim Attitudes About Important Issues
(Percent Indicating it Was Important)

COMBINED SITES	PRE-MEDIATION % N	POST-MEDIATION % N	P VALUE
Negotiating restitution	85% (153)	93% (161)	.02*
Receiving restitution	66% (155)	71% (161)	.34
Receiving answers/info	79% (157)	90% (167)	.007*
Telling offender effect	79% (157)	91% (166)	.003*
Receiving apology	70% (157)	78% (166)	.12

*Finding of significant difference

For offenders, there were no significant differences between the pre- and post-mediation samples. Negotiating restitution, paying restitution, telling the victim what happened and apologizing to the victim were important to nine of ten offenders in both samples.

Table 12 does not, however, fully capture the impact that mediation had on the offenders. Being held personally accountable for their criminal behavior often triggered a significant change in the attitude of the offender, as expressed in the following statements. "After meeting the victim I now realize that I hurt them a lot...to understand how the victim feels makes me different." Through mediation "I was able to understand a lot about what I did...I realized that the victim really got hurt and that made me feel really bad." The importance of this change in the attitude of many offenders who participated in mediation was reflected in a statement by a judge in the Oakland area. He claims that the main impact of victim-of-fender mediation on young offenders is "a major learning experience for kids about the rights of others, with implications far beyond just the delinquent act."

Table 12: Offenders' Attitudes About Important Issues
(Percent Indicating it Was Important)

COMBINED SITES	PRE-MEDIATION % N	POST-MEDIATION % N	P VALUE
Negotiating restitution	94% (138)	90% (130)	.30
Paying restitution	84% (139)	90% (128)	.20
Telling victim what happened	93% (140)	90% (137)	.40
Apologizing to victim	88% (144)	89% (134)	.50

°Finding of significant difference

6. Quality of Justice Impact: Client Satisfaction and Perceptions of Fairness

- *Mediation had a significant impact on increasing victim satisfaction with juvenile justice system.*
- *90% of victims were satisfied with the mediation outcome.*
- *91% of offenders satisfied with the mediation outcome.*
- *Victims who participated in a mediation session with their offender were significantly more likely to have experienced fairness in the justice system than were similar victims who were not in mediation.*
- *83% of victims in mediation experienced fairness in the manner in which their case was handled by the justice system.*
- *89% of offenders in mediation experienced fairness in the manner in which their case was handled by the justice system.*
- *Nearly all victims and offenders indicated that their mediator was fair.*

CLIENT SATISFACTION

The data that emerged from all four of the program sites in this study indicate high levels of participant satisfaction with the victim-offender mediation process. It is clear that from a consumer perspective, these mediation programs receive high marks. Such high levels of client satisfaction are consistent with other prior research related to victim-offender mediation, as well as the larger field of mediation in other settings.

As noted in Figure 12, victims' involvement in a face-to-face mediation session with their offender had a significant impact on increasing their satisfaction with how the juvenile justice system responded to their case, as compared to those victims who were referred to mediation but did not participate (comparison group #1) or similar victims who were never referred to mediation (comparison group #2). While 79% of victims in the mediation group indicated satisfaction, 57% in the referred-but-no-mediation group and only 57% of victims in the non-referral-to-mediation group indicated satisfaction. These findings are significant at the .05 level.

Figure 12: Victim Satisfaction
(Case Processing by Justice System)

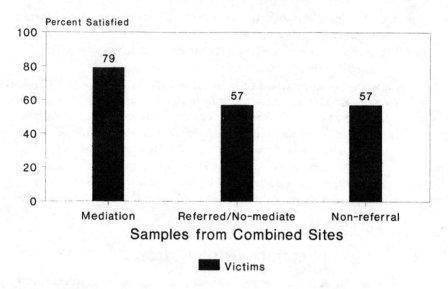

Mediation: N=204
Referred/No-Mediation: N=95
Non-Referral: N=104

When asked what they found to be the most satisfying about the face-to-face mediation session with their offender, victims expressed a number of themes. A victim in Albuquerque states that it was important for her "to find out what happened, to hear his story about why he did it and how he did it." This greater sense of satisfaction is reflected in statements by victims at the other programs such as "it gave us a chance to see each other face-to-face and to resolve what happened," or "it reduced my fear as a victim because I was able to see that they were young people," or "I feel good about it because it worked out well, because I think the kid finally realized the impact of what happened and that's not what he wants to do with himself."

A victim in Minneapolis stated that "mediation provided a quicker way and a community-based solution to the problem." "It made me feel less like a victim, but still a victim...it made me feel better about the incident." Frequently the victim's satisfaction was directly related to the mediator. "The mediator was very competent and experienced with this type of thing...when they left we were all happy." "The mediators were most helpful and sensitive to our needs."

The small portion of victims who were not satisfied with the mediation process often made comments like "the kids got off a little too easy," or "the mediator was more concerned with the offender than with the victim," or "I was led to believe that I had to go through the program to get my money."

At each of the individual program sites, mediation had a considerable impact upon increasing victim satisfaction with the justice system (see Figure 13). This impact was found to be statistically significant for both

Figure 13: Victim Satisfaction by Site
(Case Processing by Justice System)

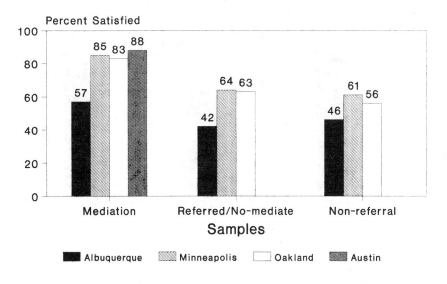

Mediation: N=204
Referred/No-Mediation: N=95
Non-Referral: N=104

comparison groups at the Minneapolis site, but only for comparison group #1 (referred but no mediation) at the Oakland site. As noted in Figure 13, 83 to 88% of victims at all of the mediation sites except Albuquerque indicated satisfaction with how their case was handled by the juvenile justice system, including the mediation aspect. In Albuquerque, only 57% of victims indicated they were satisfied. Victims in the two comparison groups in Albuquerque also indicated considerably lower satisfaction levels (42 to 46%) than victims in the two comparison groups at the remaining two sites (56 to 63%).

Nearly eight of ten offenders in all three groups (see Figure 14) indicated that they were satisfied with how the system handled their case. While 87% of offenders in mediation indicated they were satisfied, compared with 80% of the referred-but-no-mediation offender group and 78% of the non-referral-to-mediation offender group, these differences were not statistically significant. For offenders, therefore, participation in mediation appears not to have significantly increased their satisfaction with how the juvenile justice system handled their case.

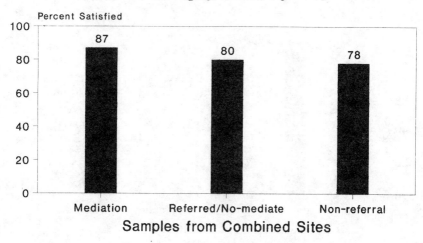

**Figure 14: Offender Satisfaction
(Case Processing by Justice System)**

Mediation: N=181
Referred/No-Mediation: N=95
Non-Referral: N=110

Satisfaction with the mediation process is captured in the following comments by juvenile offenders at the various program sites. An offender in Minneapolis states that the most satisfying thing about mediation was "I guess just to see the person, the victim and a chance to talk to him and make up for what I did." Another added, "that I could tell the victim about what happened." From the Albuquerque program, offender satisfaction was expressed by such comments as "talking to everyone got it out of my system" and "it was quickly taken care of." At the Oakland program, an offender states "mediation allowed me to get the crime off my head and to tell the victim I was sorry."

Some offenders were not, however, satisfied with how they were treated by the mediation program. Some did not like the idea of "having to go talk to those people." Several believed that they were getting "ripped off." This is well expressed by an offender in Albuquerque who stated "the guy was trying to cheat me...he was coming up with all these lists of items he claimed I took."

Juvenile offenders were consistently quite satisfied with the mediation process in all four cities. In none of the sites, however, did mediation have a significant impact upon increasing offender satisfaction with the justice system (see Figure 15) when compared to either similar offenders who were referred to mediation but who did not participate or to a matched sample of offenders from the same jurisdiction that were never referred to mediation. While the mediation program was rated highly by offenders, the other interventions offered by the local juvenile court were also rated highly. Nearly all of the juvenile offenders in the two comparison groups were in structured restitution programs that were administered by the court and that did not include mediation.

Juvenile offenders and their victims were quite satisfied with the actual outcome of the mediation session, which was nearly always a written restitution agreement. Nine of ten victims and offenders at all of the sites combined were satisfied. A frequent theme among offenders is expressed by the statement "it was helpful to see the victim as a person and to have a chance to talk with them and make up for what I did." As Figure 16 indicates, there were slight differences found between individual sites, with the most notable being a lower rate of satisfaction with the mediation outcome at the Albuquerque program site.

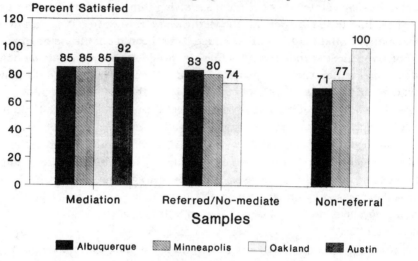

Figure 15: Offender Satisfaction by Site
(Case Processing by Justice System)

Mediation: N=181
Referred/No-Mediation: N=95
Non-Referral: N=110

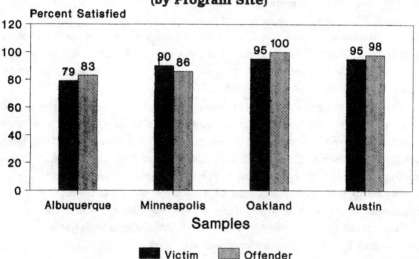

Figure 16: Satisfaction with Outcome of Mediation Session
(by Program Site)

Albuquerque: Vic. N=42, Off. N=42
Minneapolis: Vic. N=80, Off. N=59
Oakl:Vic=42,Off=34 Aust:Vic=40,Off=45

The high level of client satisfaction was not only directed toward the outcome of the mediation session or how the case was handled by the juvenile justice system. Both victims and offenders were also quite satisfied with their specific mediator. As Figure 17 indicates, 58% of victims (combined sites) were "very satisfied" and 37% were "satisfied" with their mediator, representing a total of 95% satisfaction with the mediator's performance. For offenders (combined sites), 40% were "very satisfied" and 48% were "satisfied" with their mediator, for a total satisfaction rating of 88%.

Figure 17: Satisfaction with Mediator

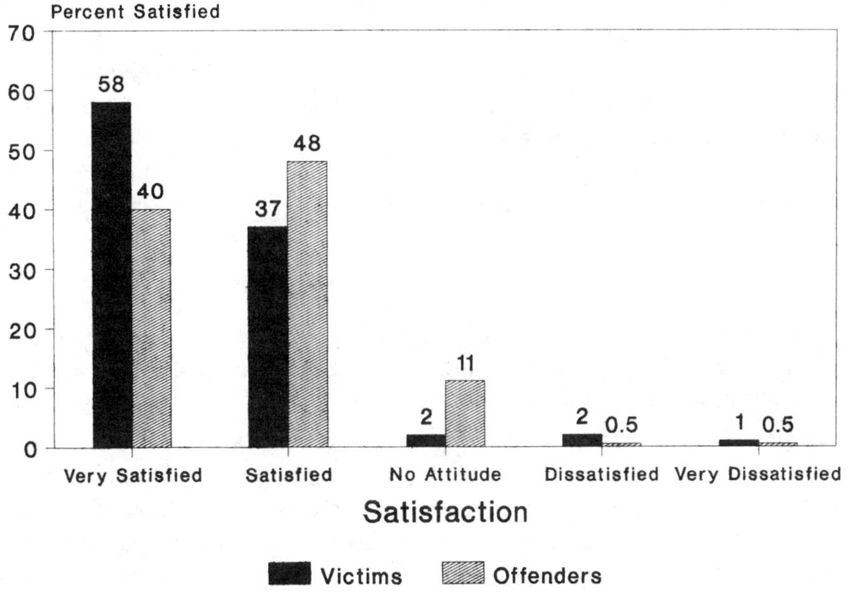

Percent Satisfied

Satisfaction

■ Victims   ▨ Offenders

(Combined Sites)

In regard to their mediator's performance, victims (combined sites) identified the following as the most important mediator tasks:

(1) Providing leadership
(2) Making victims feel comfortable
(3) Helping with restitution plan
(4) Allowing victims and offenders to talk

Juvenile offenders identified the following as the most important mediator tasks:

(1) Making offenders feel comfortable
(2) Allowing victims and offenders to talk
(3) Helping with restitution plan
(4) Being a good listener

CLIENT PERCEPTIONS OF FAIRNESS

The process of mediating conflict between crime victims and offenders is deeply rooted in the concept of offering an intervention that is perceived as fair to both parties. Examining both the meaning of fairness to victims and offenders in mediation and whether it was experienced was an important component of this cross-site study. This chapter will report on the primary concerns of victims and offenders related to fairness, the degree to which participants experienced fairness in the manner in which the juvenile justice system responded to their case, and the degree to which victims and offenders thought the mediator and the mediation outcome were fair to one or both parties.

THOUGHTS ABOUT FAIRNESS

When crime victims who participated in mediation were asked to rank their most important concerns related to fairness in the justice system, they identified "to [provide] help for the offender" as the primary concern, consistent with a prior study (Umbreit, 1988). This was followed by "to pay back the victim for their losses" and "to receive an apology from the offender." The primary victim concern of helping the offender is well-expressed by a victim in Oakland: "The only thing I want to see is that these kids receive some counseling or other type of help. I don't want to see them go to juvenile hall or prison. In counseling, the offenders would at least learn something from this." The importance of offenders being held accountable, through compensating the victim, is captured in the comments of a victim in Minneapolis. "I don't think fairness means punishment. It means restitution and responsibility. I want to give him an opportunity to make right what he's wronged. And to do this in a way that is not degrading or humiliating or vengeful, but in a way he can feel good about himself, take responsibility and correct the things he damaged."

Juvenile offenders in mediation indicated that "to pay back the victim for their losses" was their most important concern related to fairness in the justice system. The importance of this theme was captured well by an offender in Oakland who said "fairness means having a chance to work it out and pay back the victim...I feel terrible about what I did." Other concerns related to fairness were "to personally make things right," followed by "to apologize to the victim." Said an offender in St. Paul, MN, "when you do something wrong, then you have to make it right."

Figure 18: Ranking of Thoughts About Fairness

CRIME VICTIMS IN MEDIATION
(1) Providing help for the offender.
(2) Paying back the victim for losses.
(3) Receiving an apology from the offender.

JUVENILE OFFENDERS IN MEDIATION
(1) Paying back the victim for losses.
(2) Personally "making things right."
(3) Offering an apology to the victim.

EXPERIENCE OF FAIRNESS WITHIN JUSTICE SYSTEM

The aggregated data from all three primary sites indicate that the mediation process was significantly more likely to result in a perception by victims that cases were handled fairly by the juvenile justice system. As Figure 19 indicates, 83% of victims in the mediation group stated they experienced fairness in the processing of their case, compared to only 53% in the referred-but-no-mediation group and 62% in the non-referral-to-mediation group. With the growing concern to address the needs of crime victims and to more actively involve them in the justice process, this is a particularly important finding. It also indicates that the entire juvenile justice system receives credit for this increased perception of fairness— and therefore benefits from it—even though it was the mediation intervention specifically that led to this perception.

When compared to similar offenders who were never referred to the mediation program, juveniles who met their victim in mediation were also significantly more likely to indicate that they experienced fairness in the processing of their case by the juvenile justice system. Figure 20 indicates that for offenders in mediation, 89% indicated they experienced fairness, compared to 78% in the non-referral-to-mediation group. When compared to other juveniles who were referred to the mediation program but who did not participate, however, no statistically significant difference was found in their experience of fairness in the processing of their case by the system.

**Figure 19: Victim Fairness Perceptions
(Case Processing by Justice System)**

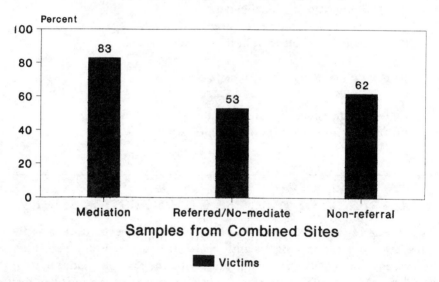

Mediation: N=204
Referred/No-Mediation: N=95
Non-Referral: N=98

When the data on perceptions of fairness were examined within program sites, rather than aggregated from combined sites, no significant differences were found among offenders. This is evidenced in Figure 21.

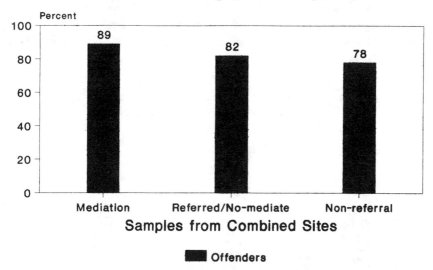

Figure 20: Offender Fairness Perceptions
(Case Processing by Justice System)

Samples from Combined Sites

Mediation: N=178
Referred/No-Mediation: N=92
Non-Referral: N=110

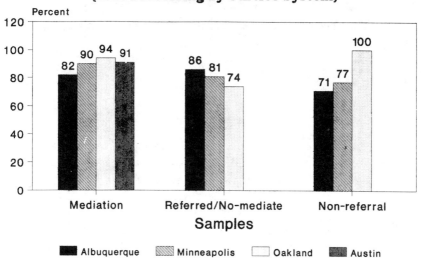

Figure 21: Offender Fairness Perceptions By Site
(Case Processing by Justice System)

Mediation: N=178
Referred/No-Mediation: N=92
Non-Referral: N=110

As noted in Figure 22, however, victims in mediation were considerably more likely to have experienced fairness at all three primary sites. Significant differences were found at the Albuquerque site (between the mediation sample and the referred/no-mediation sample) and at the Minneapolis site (between the mediation sample and both comparison groups).

**Figure 22: Victim Fairness Perceptions By Site
(Case Processing by Justice System)**

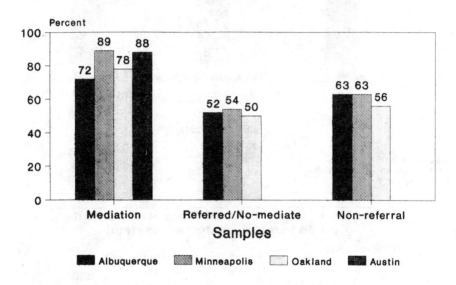

Mediation: N=204
Referred/No-Mediation: N=95
Non-Referral: N=98

For both victims and offenders at all three primary program sites, neither gender nor race was related to their experience of fairness in the manner in which the justice system responded to their case.

EXPERIENCE OF FAIRNESS WITHIN MEDIATION PROCESS

Participants in mediation overwhelmingly felt that the negotiated restitution agreement was fair to the victim. As indicated in Figure 23, nearly nine of ten victims thought the restitution agreement was fair to them, while 93% of offenders also believed the agreement was fair to the victim.

Figure 23: Fairness of Restitution Agreement to Victim in Mediation

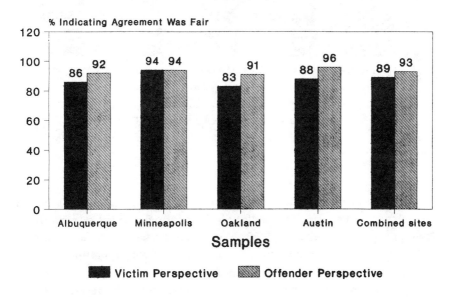

Total victims = 200
Total offenders = 167

The restitution agreements negotiated in a face-to-face mediation session between the victim and offender were also perceived as fair to the offender. Figure 24 indicates that nine of ten victims thought the agreement was fair to the offender, while 88% of offenders thought it was fair to them.

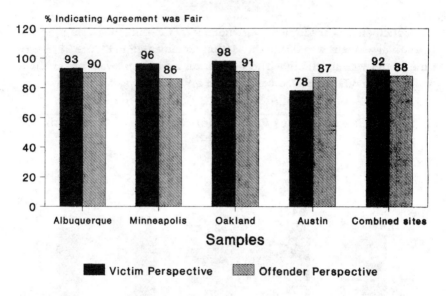

Figure 24: Fairness of Restitution Agreement to the Offender in Mediation

% Indicating Agreement was Fair

Total victims = 199
Total offenders = 175

The role of the mediator can have a critical impact upon whether participants experience the mediation process as fair. It is clear that more than nine of ten victims and offenders felt the mediator was fair. As noted in Figure 25, there were no major differences between program sites.

The strong participant perspective that mediators were fair is expressed by the following statements from a number of victims and offenders in the various programs. "She tried to be fair with both of us...she was patient" (victim in Albuquerque). "The mediator was not biased, she was not judgmental" (victim in Minneapolis). "He listened to everyone during the meeting" (offender in Minneapolis). "They (the co-mediators) were open-minded and helped us to suggest a compromise to the victim when there was a stalemate" (offender in Oakland). For those relatively few victims who indicated that the mediator was not fair, the most likely reason was that "she took sides with the offender" or "he seemed more like an advocate for the kid." The few offenders who felt the mediator was not fair indicated he or she seemed to talk primarily with the victim: "She seemed kind of one-sided in favor of the victim."

Figure 25: Fairness of Mediator

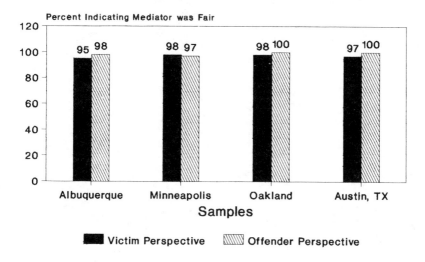

Albuquerque: Vic N=40, Off N=41
Minneapolis: Vic N=80, Off N=59
CA:Vic N=42,Off N=36   TX:Vic=38,Off=46

7. Quality of Justice Impact: Themes that Emerged from Victims and Offenders

- *Positive themes of victims*
- *Negative themes of victims*
- *Positive themes of offenders*
- *Negative themes of offenders*

While the quantitative data reported in the previous chapter are helpful in explaining how the consumers of victim-offender mediation experienced it, this chapter will present an in-depth review of the qualitative data on how victims and offenders felt and experienced the mediation process. In reviewing the vast amount of qualitative data from open-ended interviews with victims and offenders at the three primary research sites, a number of important themes emerged related to the quality of justice they perceived and experienced. The richness of qualitative data is particularly helpful in gaining a thorough and contextual understanding of the experiences and feelings of those involved in victim-offender mediation. The qualitative data clearly support the overall findings related to the positive effect of mediation on its participants. It is crucial, however, to listen to the small minority of voices expressing less favorable views of mediation. In hearing and understanding their concerns, a key may be found to further growth and development of the mediation field.

METHODOLOGY FOR QUALITATIVE DATA ANALYSIS

The methodology used to gather and analyze the qualitative data needs to be explained so the reader may understand its potential advantages and drawbacks. First, all open-ended responses were systematically recorded from the interviews of the victims and offenders, across the three sites, for the majority of post-mediation and some pre-mediation research questions. Second, the choice of questions reflects the researchers' arbitrary assessment of which questions would best uncover accurate expressions of the participants' experiences in mediation. Third, the systematized data received a cursory review, and a list was developed of positive and negative themes about the mediation experience as expressed by the respondents. Fourth, the developed themes were checked and extended with additional data reviews. Finally, random samples of 42 victims and 42 offenders were chosen, and their complete interview write-ups were thoroughly examined and checked against the developed themes.

Although there were several ways in which our analysis could have been approached, we felt that the positive-negative dichotomy was most appropriate for the preliminary stages of qualitative data analysis. This approach provided a meaningful, clear and relatively simple way of grasping the data and also opened up numerous possibilities for further analysis. A drawback to the positive-negative approach is its limited and rigid categories of positive and negative, which do not accommodate statements that are clearly neutral. This represents a legitimate concern. However, mediation—and dealing with crime in general—is a highly emotional experience, and therefore it was possible in most cases for the researcher to determine the positive or negative value of a statement by the context in which it was made. Understanding the context was essential in assigning any statement as positive or negative. Another drawback is the possibility of a researcher's bias, due to the qualitative-type data. For example, the final formulation of the themes, although based entirely on the qualitative data from the interview write-ups, was also a result of the researcher's interpretation and judgment.

A particular theme was identified in an interview write-up if it was explicitly mentioned at least once by a respondent. The results were such that the majority of themes were confirmed as representative throughout the samples, although some themes were altered and some new ones were formulated. Also, it is important to keep in mind that the list of themes is preliminary and not exhaustive. These themes also are not mutually exclusive. The number of interview schedules from the examined sample of 42 that expressed a particular theme, or its sub-theme, is presented in parentheses.

The identified themes presented in this chapter originated from the in-depth reviews of the organized data and are listed according to the frequency of their occurrence in the sample of 42 victim and 42 offender interview write-ups. Quotations that illustrate the themes are confined to this sample, except where noted. Most respondents expressed multiple themes during the interview. Therefore, the cumulative occurrence of themes is far greater than 42.

THEMES EXPRESSED BY THE VICTIMS OR OFFENDERS

The themes that were extracted through analysis of the qualitative data were divided into positive or negative based upon the viewpoints of the victim or the offender, which created four major categories. The positive themes expressed by the victim included: victim empowerment; rehabilitation of the offender; quality preparation and leadership by the mediator; receipt of restitution; and the offender looking human. The negative themes for the victim include: mediation lacking authority in assuring completion of restitution and/or inadequate punishment; dissatisfaction with mediator; offenders' uncooperative attitude; presence or absence of offender's parents in mediation; victim feeling coerced into mediation and revictimized; and inconvenience. The positive themes expressed by the offender include: dealing with feelings; achieving fairness; victim changing attitude toward offender; correcting what was done; avoiding jail/court; dealing directly with the victim; mediation session being safe/comfortable; apologizing; and being empowered through receiving a second chance. The negative themes expressed by the offender include: disempowerment/sense of injustice; grievance with other parts of the juvenile justice system; uncomfortable meeting with victim; mediators' inadequate style; punishment too small; and time span too long.

Some of the themes presented are further broken down into sub-themes. Themes are listed according to the frequency of responses from the most to the least. Also, there were other themes expressed by a particular victim or offender that were left out of this summary because of space consideration and the infrequent occurrence in the sample.

POSITIVE THEMES OF VICTIMS

Victim Empowerment (Three Sub-themes, N=42): Almost all victims expressed satisfaction with one or more aspects of personal empowerment in the process of mediation. This theme was further divided into three sub-themes: feeling involved in the process of justice, expressing opinions and/or emotions and having a sense of emotional healing.

Feeling Involved (N=19): Victims generally expressed satisfaction about participating in the process of mediation. They emphasized the human-ness of the mediation experience in which the two parties were involved, as opposed to the depersonalized court procedures. "The juvenile justice system is less humane than I thought. This program is a nice alternative." "It's a fascinating experience...it makes things more personal and more human, a rare opportunity in the world." "It makes it more personal-ized...not like the courts. It made me feel someone cared, rather than the impersonal court. It makes you feel like a person, not a number." "I was surprised I was treated like a person by the system." "The fact that we could settle it out of court gave a positive feeling to justice."

Equally frequent were statements praising the victim's active role in the justice process. "I was allowed to participate, and I felt I was able to make decisions rather than the system making them for me." "It gave me a feeling of being more involved in what's going on instead of just filing a police report...." "In mediation...you could deal with the offender, instead of the cops taking him away." "I was able to provide some input into the pay-back agreement." "The mediation made me feel like I had something to do with what went on...that justice has been served, I guess."

Victims often expressed satisfaction with having a personal impact on the offender and their future. "I liked the fact that I may be helping a young person stay away from a life of crime." "I got a chance to be a direct influence on the offender." Some victims seemed to gain satisfaction from taking the role of a judge through determining what the offender should do. "We pretty much spelled it out." "I am the one who decided the restitution."

Expressing Opinions and/or Emotions (N=13): Victims appreciated the opportunity to voice their opinions about the crime and/or the offender. "It felt good to tell him our opinion." "I got my point across." "The offender saw our side. They have to know how serious their behavior was."

Expressing emotions also seemed crucial in the mediation session. It served the purpose of further humanizing the meeting experience through the victim's healing or the impression it left on the offender. "Our express-ing emotions gave them a better understanding of the damage they have done and the lives they had affected." In this context, the mediator's empathy and counseling skills played an important role. "She did a good job of eliciting my emotions around it, making me comfortable with my emotions. She diffused my anger, labeled my feelings."

Healing (N=10): One-fourth of the victims pointed out the importance of mediation for resolving their feelings of grief and distress caused by the crime. This healing in mediation occurred in a variety of ways, as illustrated by the following quotes: "It provides a chance for healing; a chance for information sharing; a chance for building relationships instead of destroying them...it's a healing-type thing, rather than just seeking justice and punishment." "It gave me a good feeling. We were able to get over our sense of loss." "When your house is burglarized it helps to soothe some of the frustration and anxiety to know the "whys" for it, some reasons." "It (mediation) should be imperative in violent crimes, just to get an understanding, and not living the nightmare your whole life." "I liked the personalness [sic]—it made me feel less like a victim, but still a victim." "You come out and say things and release things and feel better."

Rehabilitation of the Offender (N=17): Juvenile offenders often fail to grasp the effects of their criminal acts. Mediation appears to offer them an opportunity to experience empathy for and awareness of other people's feelings, and this awareness is a crucial part of growing up and becoming a socially responsible adult. Victims' responses commonly tied the offender's rehabilitation to the offender's understanding of the effects of his or her crime on the victim—of material, as well as emotional, harm done to another person. "I'm sure he's realized the severity of what he's done and he won't do it again." "The offenders needed to see how the crime affected the customers and us." "It helps the offender to realize the humanness of the person they have offended." The victim participated in mediation "so he could know how I feel...so he won't hurt somebody else." "It's part of learning empathy...he must understand." "The kid learns and gains some empathy." "Mediation should definitely be a part of the process...to actually face the person who had to absorb what you did is a bit different than to just have to deal with the justice system...they can be pretty hard and cold against that (the system)...she seemed to really want to get this off her chest...like it had been bothering her."

Some victims were pleased to see that offenders have "straightened out." This often meant that offenders had taken responsibility for their actions and had completed the restitution. "I think it is doing the kid a lot of good...he is taking responsibility for what he's done and doing something about it." "What a pleasure seeing him come full circle...I hired him, and he is working here now." "It was a pleasure to work with this individual who was willing to take responsibility for his actions." "He was remorseful and it was apparent in what he said, and he was willing to make things right."

Generally, victims showed interest in the offenders' well-being. "The impression that I got is that somebody might get through to him. I think he can be reached." "I think he's grown from this experience." "Talking with the person who did this and seeing how much this (mediation) did help him...I think that's important."

Quality Preparation and Leadership by the Mediator (N=15): Victims frequently stressed the importance of being prepared by the mediator for the mediation session. This included familiarizing the victim with the process of mediation. "I knew what to expect, and I knew what was expected from me." With some victims it also involved being informed about the offender's background. "She told me about him, so he seemed more like a person."

The expected level of the mediator's involvement in the process varied among victims. For some, the mediator's mere presence was sufficient. "Just that I knew that I wasn't going to be alone with the kid." Other victims appreciated the mediator's guidance. "They knew what they were doing." "The mediator took genuine interest in the case...it wasn't just a job she was doing, it was something that she really wanted to do, and she had kind of a passion for it."

The importance of the mediator's attention to the victim's needs comes across in the following quotes: "The mediator made sure I was satisfied. There was good follow-through." "They definitely set up a comfortable environment for everyone involved."

Receiving Restitution (N=9): In the quantitative part of the research, approximately 70% of the victims indicated that receiving restitution was important. However, this was a less significant theme in the open-ended responses of our sample, with less than one fourth mentioning it explicitly. A few victims expressed satisfaction with receiving restitution. "We received reimbursement for our destroyed property." "It is important to get back what you lost." "We all have to pay for what we do." For some victims, restitution was important only as a gesture of the offender's admission of guilt and acceptance of responsibility for what was done. "I wanted them to show their willingness to pay me. But money wasn't important." Four victims pointed out the importance of coming to a fair agreement with the offender. "It's good to communicate the agreement in a non-hostile environment, to correct a problem, not just to punish."

Offender Looks Human (N=8): For the victim to perceive the offender as human is another important aspect of humanizing the experience of justice through the mediation process. "It minimized the fear I would have as a victim because I got to see that they were real people, diminishing the fantasy of what they would be like." Fairly common was a victim's surprise about how positive the offender looked. "I expected his attitude to be bad, but he was sorry. He needed to be hugged." "I expected a real bully...he was a clean-cut, sensitive kid."

NEGATIVE THEMES OF VICTIMS

Although a number of negative themes among victims in mediation have been identified, their frequency is quite low. For many of the criticisms it was difficult to distinguish which part of the juvenile justice system they referred to. On the one hand, some were clearly targeting parts of the system other than mediation (the police, judges, detention centers, etc.), even though the questions asked were about mediation. On the other hand, some comments were very vague and/or general. The themes listed below represent only those comments that were clearly related to mediation.

Mediation Lacking Authority in Assuring Completion of Restitution and/or Inadequate Punishment (N=10): Often, by the time of the post-mediation interview, the victim still had not received the restitution or had no information about the restitution completion. "I was not paid as was agreed, and I have not been contacted about it. I don't know what is going on." "There seems to be no mechanism to enforce the agreement made in the mediation session." "When they don't comply with the restitution, it's just a waste of everyone's time." "There was no follow-through during the time of community service." "The success of the program depends on whether the offender complies. The young man hasn't kept his bargain." "I wasn't able to follow up more quickly with the restitution."

Some victims felt that the offenders were not punished adequately. "She got off scot-free." "It wasn't severe enough...I would have liked to have had the response to the boys' actions be a little more serious." "I wasn't reimbursed enough." Some victims complained about the mediation experience not being authoritative enough for the offenders. "Mediators don't have judicial power." "Maybe, the mediation people should read from a law book or something to give examples of what would happen if the offender did this again. Offenders should be scared straight regardless of how petty the crime was." Several victims also expressed dissatisfaction over not meeting with other offenders involved in the crime.

Dissatisfaction with Mediator (Two Sub-themes, N=8): (Illustrative quotations from outside of the sample of 42 victims were used.) Dissatisfaction with the mediator generally fell into two sub-themes: the mediator's style was viewed as inadequate, or there seemed insufficient preparation by the mediator. Victims occasionally objected to the mediator's style, which could have been too passive, too directive, or routine and mechanical. The importance of an individualized and sensitive approach that is tuned into the characteristics and dynamics of each mediation experience cannot be overemphasized. The mediator's passivity, when objected to, was closely related to a sense of the mediator not being in control of the meeting and offering little leadership or direction. "He was kind of quiet. I felt like we needed more direction." "At times she wasn't in control of what was going on." Alternatively, when the mediator was perceived as too directive, it seemed that the victim usually walked away with a sense of not being heard and not being able to fully express his or her concerns. "The mediator talked a lot, without allowing for the spontaneity of the process or for moments of silence." "The mediator talked too much. The offender hardly said anything." "One of the mediators volunteered some possible solutions for restitution...he pushed too much, perhaps."

A few victims complained about mediators being routine, unprofessional or both. This was sometimes related to the victim's perception of a lack of authority in mediation, inadequate consequences for the offender and even the victim's feelings of revictimization. "The mediators were unprofessional. The program seemed shallow...the meeting was too short, and the offender needed more of a lecture or more consequences pressed." "The people from the VORP are not professional and looked very sloppy. It was like being in eighth grade. The guy (the mediator) just read off of note cards...he would have no idea of what to do if it wasn't for his note cards. It was like a canned speech. The fellow (the mediator) needed to shave, and the gal (another mediator) was wearing hippy-dippy cosmic clothes...It reminded me of a summer camp, and they were like camp counselors. The program director was better prepared and had a tie on. The other two (the mediators) he never should have let loose on us."

The mediator's competence was questioned in the following quote, which includes a sense of the victim being revictimized in the mediation session. "One of the mediators didn't have much ability, I guess. The mediator was so intimidated by the offender. He left me uncomfortable and let the offender do all the talking." One victim felt misunderstood by the mediator. "She thought this was positive, and I just wasn't feeling that way. I was so upset."

Several victims objected to not being adequately prepared for the session by the mediator. This included feeling uninformed about the process when the mediation began. "She could have told us more about the process." "I wasn't prepared for the mediators to ask me to bargain for the damage." "We should have sat down and talked about what my role was. I had a basic idea, but I had the impression that she (the mediator) wanted more than what I did."

Offenders' Non-Cooperative Attitude (N=6): Disappointment with the offender's attitude is illustrated by the following statements: "He had a real poor attitude." "I don't think he cares about his actions." "It wasn't done well. The offender was so aggressive." "I didn't find out the reason why she stole my check. She just said 'I don't know.'" "The kid sat and argued and said he didn't do it. We argued back and forth. I left so I wouldn't hit the kid in the face." In the last situation, it was the mediator's job to prevent or stop that arguing. This quote points out the need for more rigorous mediator selection and training, but also exemplifies the extremely difficult situations in which mediators often find themselves.

Presence or Absence of Offenders' Parents in Mediation (N= 6): Victims also complained about parents being present. "I would insist mothers not attend." "I was very upset about their dad's attitude." "It was friendly between myself and the kids. Parents were a pain." Parents often demanded harder punishment for their children. "There should be better control over parents...one of them made it very difficult on everyone, especially her son." Or, parents assumed a defense position for a child. "Parents shouldn't be able to interrupt; his father was protecting him." On the other side, victims occasionally stated a necessity of parents being present in mediation session. "Their parents should be there; it should be a requirement. These guys are juveniles."

Victim Felt Coerced into Mediation and Revictimized (N=6): (Illustrative quotations were used from outside of the sample of 42 victims.) As previously mentioned, one of the basic principles of mediation is that the victim's participation is absolutely voluntary. However, a small number of victims did feel forced to participate in mediation. One victim thought that there was no other way of receiving restitution. "I was led to believe I had to go through the program to get my money." Another victim felt a burden of responsibility for the offender's future. "I think I should have been reimbursed in total. I was pressured into accepting something lower. I was actually scared that the kid's future was on the line with my whole decision. Because, had I asked for the full estimated cost, the mediator said that the boys would be charged with felony, which meant that they would lose their driver's license, and the possibility of getting into some schools and into the armed forces would be reduced for them." It is hard to imagine anything more disturbing for the victim than feeling victimized again in the mediation session. When this occurs, all empowerment efforts of mediation are completely undermined.

Feelings of re-victimization are often experienced in connection with feeling coerced into mediation (the victim's perception of participating in mediation on a non-voluntary basis). This can also be a consequence of the offender's attitude. "They tended to downplay the actual damages." "They were lying and we had to listen."

Feelings of re-victimization also resulted from a perception of the mediator as biased toward the offender. "It was my impression that the mediators thought I was driving too hard a deal." "They were concerned more with the offender than with the victim." "I feel like I am being treated as the offender because of this meeting and everything. It's all a waste of time." "Well, basically, whenever you are dealing with a juvenile, you go in it with them [the mediators] treating you more like you did it, than [like you are] the victim. It just seems like there are so many more burdens on you than on the person who did it."

These findings have important implications for mediator training. Both parties, and especially the victim, need to be informed about all available options. They need to learn of the potential benefits and drawbacks of mediation in an objective, unbiased way. It should be the mediator's primary task to assure that the choice of the victim and offender to participate is an informed one. In addition, training must emphasize the importance of mediators providing introductory comments on their neutrality, and to follow up by actually not taking sides. It also needs to provide mediators with sensitivity to each victim and his or her needs. Mediation's main strength is its ability to personalize and humanize the justice process. If the individual needs of victims are ignored, mediation cannot be successful.

POSITIVE THEMES OF OFFENDERS

Dealing with Feelings (Four Sub-themes, N=53): This is a fairly complex theme expressed by offenders related to their satisfaction with mediation. It involved offenders expressing their feelings and their side of the story, learning about victims' feelings, feeling cared about, and making a victim feel better.

Expressing Feelings (N=27): Many offenders described an almost cathartic relief of having their feelings expressed. Combined with expressing opinions and telling victims their side of the story, this theme was expressed by two-thirds of our sample of 42 offenders. It seemed that being involved with crime was a fairly traumatic experience for most juvenile offenders (for some, perhaps, this relates to being caught in the crime), which creates a diversity of emotions in a young person. For some, mediation clearly helped in dealing with these emotions. "It made me happy, because all my feelings were out." "I got off my chest what I had to say." "It made me feel a lot better after talking, because I was down about what I did. I learned my lesson. I was hanging around with a wrong crowd."

Even more often than expressing their feelings, young offenders talked about welcoming the chance to tell the victim their side of the story. "It felt good telling him exactly what happened and how." "By telling them what happened, they can understand what you are about." "You get your side of a story in."

One component of the relief experienced by offenders may be the frequently mentioned satisfaction that the whole crime experience can be placed behind them. Mediation appeared to have contributed to a sense of closure for the offender. "This is in the past now. It's over." "I got it off my mind, and I know I don't have to worry about it any more." It is possible that a sense of relief occurred in some offenders because of their uncertainty and fear of consequences of their crime. Once the mediation session was over and they had met the victim, their fear of an angry and demanding victim diminished. "I always thought they were out to get you... this program shows that they want to help you."

Learning About the Victims' Feelings (N=12): Learning about the victims' feelings was often emphasized as an important and sometimes surprising experience. Finding out that a victim is a human being with feelings appeared to create a shift in a young person's perspective on the crime, which until then was depersonalized. "It was helpful to get their point of view and to be put in their shoes." "You get to see their feelings about it." Establishing in a young person a connection between his or her actions and another person's direct hurt may be crucial for reducing recidivism. "It is very unlikely that I will commit another crime; I realize that I've hurt the victim a lot." "To understand how the victim feels makes me feel different." "I was able to understand a lot about what I did. I realized that the victim really got hurt and that made me feel really bad." "All the programs that I am working on now help me to think about the victim and to think twice." "After this, it got to my mind that it's kind of stupid to do stuff like that. Talking to the victim really changes a lot ... this guy uses his truck for work."

Being Understood and Cared About (N=8): A surprising number of offenders expressed good feelings about being understood and even cared about by their victims and mediators. "Seeing she (the victim) could be understanding made me feel really good." "It (mediation) makes the victim understand you." "They showed some good qualities toward me and they cared about me." Many others expressed this theme implicitly.

Making the Victim Feel Better (N=6): This is related to correcting what has been done in the crime, hoping for a softer punishment, and is part of an offender's empowerment. "It felt good knowing that the victim felt better after talking about it." "The meeting was very helpful to the victim; I could see it from their eyes." "Once I got caught I knew I was wrong, and I wanted to do everything I could to make it good for him."

Fairness (N=20): In most cases, offenders perceived mediation as being fair, with about half explicitly mentioning it. "I liked the fairness of it." "Everything in this program was perfect. Everything in this program was fair. This program totally shocked me. It was a real relief. I am glad there is this program." "Juvenile justice is more fair than I thought before."

Many were pleasantly surprised by the punishment, because they initially expected it to be stricter. "I didn't get punished too strongly." "I didn't get in that much trouble." "For what I did, I feel I got pretty fair treatment." "Just enough for what I did." Some were also surprised by the positive attitude of victims toward them. "I wasn't sure how the victims were going to react and I was expecting worse." "I was surprised by how he reacted toward me. I thought he was going to be all mad, but he wasn't. I didn't think the mediation was going to be that friendly."

Fairness was perceived by some offenders as passively happening to them. For others, actively working out a fair settlement directly with victims, through mediation, seemed to be a very important component of their understanding of fairness. "We got to work it out together." "We were able to compromise and work things out." "Everything was worked out; there weren't any hostile disagreements." "In mediation we get to work it out and everything gets settled." "The hatchet is buried and it is put to rest."

Victim Changing Attitude toward Offender (N=18): What the victim thinks of the offender was very important to almost half of our sample of 42 offenders. "The most satisfying was to have them like me, to have them know who I am. To be friends." "I didn't want her to think bad things about me." "I wanted to let them know I am not a bad person, I just made a mistake." "I didn't want her to think bad things about me." "I am sure she thought we were hoodlums until we talked." "Before, he thought I was a lowlife." "I wanted...to have them like me, to have them know who I am, to be friends."

Correcting What Was Done (N=17): Related to the victim's attitude toward them was the offender's need to make things right, to correct what was done to the victim. "Restitution is a top priority and I am doing everything I can to pay it back." "I felt this was my responsibility (the restitution) and the least I could do." "I had a chance of doing something to correct what I did without having to pay bad consequences." "I was able to work instead of paying a fine, and it felt good to do it. I showed that I could do something good. It was a fair way to work it out. It helped me a lot."

Obviously, some offenders used the experience of mediation for improving their own lives. This may be another way in which mediation has a positive impact on reducing further criminal behavior. "It made me think a little bit about my life...I don't want to be getting into trouble again." "Things eat at me inside, and I needed to take care of them." "Now I'm doing better about everything I do; people treat me better." "I would recommend mediation to other offenders because they might feel better about themselves, and I think it would help them stop stealing. I am glad we did it. It helped me stop stealing. I'd be stealing more stuff, bigger stuff. I'd be in more trouble." "Now I know more, I know how to control myself." "I do have to work to pay everything back. And I do have to talk about my problems in counseling."

Avoiding Jail and Court (N=13): A large number of offenders appreciated mediation because they were not sent to jail or to court. "I am glad they didn't send me to Totem Town." "Nothing goes on my record." "We were able to settle it out of court." "I didn't have to go to court." "It's better than either of the other choices..." "I am glad I didn't go to jail, because I don't want this to effect my chances to become a fireman."

Dealing Directly with the Victim (N=9): Some offenders emphasized the importance of direct communication with a victim. "That way we can talk up front, not behind each other's back." "I think that was a good idea to tell him in person." "To let him know why we did it, the reason for it, so he didn't have to think, 'Did they hate me?'" "I got to meet with the victims and talk with them, rather than going to juvenile hall and doing nothing." "It's the best way to resolve things. You get things resolved in a real way. It's better than doing time."

Mediation Session Being Safe/Comfortable (N=9): Offenders generally didn't expect the session to be pleasant, but a number of them were surprised at experiencing it as safe and comfortable. "... the comfortable-ness that I felt while there." "The meeting was safe, under control." "That way (in mediation), the victims aren't able to do any cussing or say anything bad." "I feel safer now (after mediation); I have to pass their house on my way to the store." This theme seems connected with the victim's positive attitude toward the offender, receiving a chance to make things right and feeling cared about.

The mediator's skills and style played an important role. "He (the mediator) was quiet. You felt he wasn't there, but you knew he was." "It was her first time and she was great."

Apologizing (N=7): Having the opportunity to apologize to the victim for their behavior was often seen by offenders as one of the main benefits of mediation. "It was a good way of apologizing to the victim." "I liked being able to apologize. To let him know that we are not bad." "Apologizing made me feel better and then I knew it was settled." "'Cause then, you have feelings about what you did. Apologizing brings out feelings."

Empowerment through Receiving a Chance (N=7): Being cared about and understood by a victim seemed inseparable from receiving a chance to make things right and being respected in the process of mediation. Many offenders strongly emphasized these points and obviously felt empowered by the mediation experience. "You felt you had some say-so." "I got a chance to have a say in my punishment." "They listened to good stuff I'm doing now." "They were courteous and listened to me." "In mediation, offenders can see that there is hope; instead of going and getting into tons of trouble, there's a different way." "They were trying to help me out, [to help me] stay out of court. It helped me to get back to how I used to be. Like, doing what I am supposed to do and get me back to school."

NEGATIVE THEMES OF OFFENDERS

Feeling Disempowered/A Sense of Injustice (Three Sub-themes, N=28):
Some offenders felt they had to agree to an unjust restitution. "The
restitution was too much." "I took only one thing from the house. There
was one offender who took about 20 things, and he got the same punishment as I did." "I had to pay too much."

Occasionally, such an offender expressed opinions about and feelings
of being wrongly accused. "I was sent to a detention home. They said I was
the offender, and I don't feel that was right." "She accused me of doing it,
and I didn't do it." These offenders periodically communicated their
perception that a victim took advantage of them. "He lied about the
damages." "I am just mad that she got more money than she originally
had." "He was trying to throw a fast one on me." "The guy was trying to
cheat me; he was coming up with all these lists." "She accused me of doing
it because they said they saw someone tall, but I didn't do it." "I thought
we had to pay too much money. It was nice that they weren't mad and we
got it over with, but I also think they took advantage of us."

Dissatisfaction with the Mediator (N=12): Objections by the offender to
the style of the mediator stem from it being perceived as passive, routine
and/or insecure. When the mediator was perceived as too passive, offenders felt they were not able to express themselves. Some even felt threatened. This seemed especially true when the victim was perceived as
overpowering: "She didn't lead. She was like a ghost." "I would have wanted
them to answer my questions, but the mediator didn't help." Sometimes,
the mediator's passivity was viewed as a strength. This was particularly
so when an agreement was reached, and the tone of the meeting was
friendly: "The mediator beforehand just gave us a brief understanding of
how it would work and then after that pretty much didn't have to do
anything. We talked and worked out an agreement." A few offenders were
dissatisfied with the mediator acting in what they perceived to be a routine
and mechanical manner. "...Leading the conversation for what they
wanted to hear, for the paperwork, or something." Some mediators were
perceived by the offenders as being insecure. "They were a little bit
confused about what they wanted to say. They would start saying something, and then would change it and say something else." "It was their first
meeting. They seemed a little hesitant."

Several offenders felt that they were not listened to. They blamed this on the mediator. "I didn't feel my side was expressed enough." "The mediators never asked us our opinion about restitution." "The mediators didn't allow us to talk directly with the victims." "He (the mediator) seemed kind of one-sided toward another party." "I think they sided a bit with the victim." When expressing dissatisfaction about not being listened to, most offenders referred to their opinion about restitution being inadequately considered. Yet, a small number of them referred to the sense that their interpretation of the crime was not respected. "I needed to express my side. I really wish she had listened."

Being Overly Criticized by the Victim (N=6): "The victim kept telling me I did wrong and how bad I was....The lady kept telling me I was incorrect. I'd like her to mellow out a bit." "...Having to listen to them putting us down." "I didn't like the way the kids criticized me." "After the meeting one of the victims was a real jerk. I went to shake his hand and say I was sorry, and he just walked away." "They kept putting us down and saying that we shouldn't be able to see each other. They weren't much worth talking with. When I've been seeing them drive by, all I get is a dirty look." "One of the victims called us and cussed us out on the phone."

Grievance with Other Parts of Juvenile Justice System (N= 6): Some offenders made obvious their dissatisfaction with other aspects of the juvenile justice system, or with the system in general. "I didn't like how the people at the juvenile detention center treated people...they view them all as guilty and treat them like crap...they yell at people...they don't let you express your side of the story. But I thought the whole mediation process was really good." "The detention home was the worst." "Everyone in this system treated me like shit!" "The cops caught me and beat me up." "I didn't like the cops walking in my house when I told them not to." "In the court I didn't understand nothing [sic], and nothing was explained to me. Kids don't know what's going on."

Uncomfortable Meeting (N=6): For a number of offenders, the mediation session wasn't a place where they felt comfortable. Some didn't feel mediation was their choice. A perceived blame by the victim, and self-blame, are both obvious in offenders' responses. "I felt like dirt. I could tell he had some resentment. His resentment was only natural. I was really nervous." "Having to meet with him was rather uncomfortable." "It was sort of tense in there." "It was kind of hard to sit there and look him in the eye and tell him I broke into his car." "I wasn't real comfortable at first...I felt kind of awkward because he was a real nice guy, and sitting there knowing that I had done something to his car wasn't a good feeling." One offender, who probably had anticipated something very unpleasant, felt uncomfortable at first but as the session progressed became more relaxed. "The first couple of minutes was uncomfortable, 'cause you didn't know how it was going."

CONCLUSION

A portion of the vast amount of qualitative data collected in this study has been summarized. The potential for additional qualitative analysis of the data is enormous. The analysis presented in this chapter is preliminary and exploratory. It remains on the level of generating ideas and insights into victims' and offenders' experiences in mediation.

The data revealed that the great majority of participants were satisfied with mediation and considered it to be a positive experience. Therefore, it can be concluded that mediation between victims and juvenile offenders does meet many needs of the parties involved. However, since this field is young and growing, a special effort was made during this study to elicit criticisms and ideas for improvement from the clients. This was summarized through negative themes expressed by victims and offenders.

The relatively equal number of positive and negative themes is not reflective of the distribution within the data, since the data are overwhelmingly positive. Rather, it reflects our efforts to develop an understanding of the possibilities for further growth and improvement of the humanizing and empowering practice of mediation.

NOTE: The initial data analysis and draft of this chapter were prepared by Boris Kalanj, MSW, who served as a research assistant for the study. Mr. Kalanj is currently a doctoral student in the School of Social Work at the University of Minnesota.

8. Mid-Range Outcomes: Restitution Completion and Recidivism

- *Victims were significantly more likely to actually receive restitution if they participated in a mediation session with their offender.*
- *Juvenile offenders were held more accountable for successful completion of their restitution obligation through victim-offender mediation programs.*
- *Juvenile offenders in mediation programs committed considerably fewer crimes than a matched sample of similar offenders not in mediation*
- *This finding of lower recidivism, however, was not statistically significant.*

RESTITUTION COMPLETION

An important outcome of the victim-offender mediation process is a written restitution plan negotiated by the victim and offender. For the combined sites, 95% of mediations (as noted in Chapter 5) resulted in a successfully negotiated restitution agreement that was considered fair to both parties.

The importance of victims being compensated for their losses through some form of restitution (i.e., financial, personal service to victim or community service) is highlighted in the following statements: "Getting paid back was real important because I was in a very bad financial situation at the time." "The money was not important, but it was very important that the offender worked off the time, and that she had done something that was of benefit to me." "He owes me that." Restitution is increasingly being required of juvenile offenders in many courts throughout the U.S. The more important issue, however, is whether restitution is actually completed by the offender. For victims to have their expectations raised by court-ordered restitution, yet to later never receive compensation by the offender, could lead to a "second victimization" experience.

In order to examine the issue of successful restitution completion by juvenile offenders, court data related to actual completion of restitution were analyzed at the Minneapolis and Albuquerque program sites. Data were not available at the Austin and Oakland sites because of limited resources, and the manner in which such information was reported and stored by the local juvenile court.

The comparison groups for this analysis represented a sample of similar offenders from same jurisdiction who were matched with the offenders in mediation on the variables of age, race, sex, offense and amount of restitution (within $100). In Hennepin County (Minneapolis area), only post-adjudication mediation cases and their matched comparison group were examined. Data were not available in the court records on restitution completion for pre-adjudication diversion cases. In Albuquerque, both pre- and post-adjudication mediation cases and their matched comparison group were examined.

While the Center for Victim Offender Mediation in Minneapolis serves both Hennepin (Minneapolis area) and Ramsey (St. Paul area) counties, the vast majority of cases are from Hennepin County. Therefore, the analysis of restitution completion focused exclusively on Hennepin County. In addition to matching the comparison group sample along the above-mentioned variables, the Hennepin County analysis of restitution completion also controlled for time, by measuring restitution completion by either the mediation sample or the comparison group within a one-year period. This was not possible at the Albuquerque site.

The unit of measurement in Hennepin County was that of "restitution agreements" rather than simply the offender, who may have had several restitution agreements since multiple victims were involved. By examining completion of each victim-offender agreement, even if the same offender was involved in several agreements, it was believed that a more accurate analysis could occur. For example, if one offender had negotiated three different restitution agreements with three different victims, failure to pay all but $10 of one of the agreements would be measured as non-completion if the unit of measurement were the offender, even though he or she successfully completed two other restitution agreements. Conversely, if the unit of measurement is the restitution agreement, this offender would have registered one non-completion and two successfully completed restitution obligations. Use of the restitution agreement as the unit of measurement occurred only at the Minneapolis site for Hennepin County data on post-adjudication cases.

In both Albuquerque and Minneapolis, there were highly structured court-administered restitution programs for all those juvenile offenders with a restitution responsibility, with the exception of a smaller group that was referred to the local victim-offender mediation program. This is important because a more informal process of judges periodically ordering restitution, without the presence of a structured program and staff to monitor completion, would likely result in far fewer successful completions of restitution than the court-administered programs from which the comparison group samples were drawn.

Figure 26: Restitution Completion
(Mediation and Matched Comparison Group)

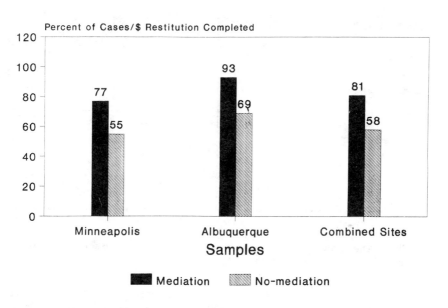

Combined Mediation: N=167
Combined No Mediation N=221

As Table 13 indicates, offenders who negotiated restitution agreements with their victims through a process of mediation were significantly more likely to actually complete their restitution obligation than similar offenders who were ordered by the court to pay a set amount of restitution. At the Minneapolis site (Hennepin County), 77% of juvenile offenders in the victim-offender mediation program successfully completed their restitution obligation, compared to only 55% of similar offenders (matched sample) in the court-administered restitution program, which did not include a mediation session with the victim. In Albuquerque, 93% of the juvenile offenders in the victim-offender mediation program successfully completed their restitution obligation to the victim, compared to 69% of similar offenders (matched sample) who were in the court-administered restitution program involving no mediation.

Table 13: Restitution Completion by Offenders
(Percent of Restitution Completed)

SAMPLE	MINNEAPOLIS % N	ALBUQUERQUE % N	TOTAL % N
Mediation Sample (experimental group)	77% (125)	93% (42)	81% (167)
Non-Referral Matched Sample (comparison group)	55% (179)	69% (42)	58% (221)
Probability of chance	p=.0001*	p=.005*	p=.0001*

* Finding of significant difference
NOTE: The Minneapolis sample was based upon total restitution agreements, after offenders were matched.

When the Albuquerque and Minneapolis program sites are combined, 81% of offenders in the victim-offender mediation program successfully completed restitution, compared to 58% of similar offenders who did not negotiate a restitution plan directly with their victim through the mediation process. All of these differences, at both the individual and combined sites, are statistically significant. This significantly higher rate of restitution completion may well be related to a greater sense of "ownership" of the restitution responsibility that is experienced by offenders in mediation. It may also be related to the fact that the actual restitution amount and form is likely to be more realistic as a result of the direct face-to-face negotiation between the parties.

A previous study by Schneider and Schneider (1984) found that victims of crime were more likely to receive restitution from juvenile offenders who were involved in a structured "programmatic" restitution program, rather than an "ad-hoc" restitution program of the court. Prior to this cross-site analysis of victim-offender mediation, no study has ever examined the impact of face-to-face mediation on successful completion of restitution. The finding that mediation has a significant impact is critical. At a time when concern for serving the needs of crime victims continues to grow, the fact that victim-offender mediation can significantly increase the likelihood of victims being compensated, in some form, for their losses has very important implications for juvenile justice policymakers and those concerned with serving victims of crime.

Table 14: Characteristics of Minneapolis Mediation Sample (N=87) and Matched Comparison Sample (N=87)

CHARACTERISTIC	OCCURRENCE	PERCENT
AGE Mean age of 16		100
GENDER		
Female	9	10
Male	78	90
RACE		
White	73	84
Black	7	8
Native American	5	6
Asian	2	2
CHARGE		
Burglary	35	40
Damage to Property	16	19
Theft	12	14
Unauthorized use of motor vehicle	11	13
Forgery	3	4
Assault	2	2
Stolen Property	2	2
Tampering	2	2
Arson	1	1
Hit and Run	1	1
Negligent Fires	1	1
Robbery	1	1

Tables 14 and 15 provide additional data related to the Minneapolis site, which represented the far larger sample and at which more extensive data were available. Characteristics of the mediation and matched sample in Hennepin County are presented first, followed by the total dollars of restitution paid by both samples and the average (mean) amount of restitution for both samples.

Table 15: Dollar Completion of Restitution Within One Year

	MEDIATION SAMPLE		NO-MEDIATION SAMPLE	
	$	%	$	%
Complete	$20,225	80%	$13,244	53%
Incomplete	$5,072	20%	$11,828	47%
Total Obligation	$25,297	100%	$25,072	100%
Mean	$290.77		$288.18	
Standard Deviation	266.32		263.74	
Coefficient of Relative Variance	.9159		.9152	

RECIDIVISM

Victim-offender mediation staff and volunteers are often asked about whether the program has an impact on reducing further criminal behavior (recidivism) by those offenders participating in mediation. The issue of recidivism was examined at all of the three initial sites.

Recidivism was defined as commission of a new criminal offense within a one-year period in which there was an admission of guilt and a response by the justice system, even if the disposition hearing occurred outside the one-year time frame. For offenders in mediation, the time frame was one year from the date of the mediation session. For the comparison group, the time frame was one year from the court disposition for the offense that was matched with the mediation sample. Status offenses, probation violations and charges that were dismissed were not included as "recidivism."

The comparison group at each site consisted of similar offenders from the same jurisdiction who were matched with offenders in mediation along the variables of age, sex, race, offense and restitution amount. These offenders were involved in structured, court-administered restitution programs that did not include a face-to-face mediation session with victims.

Figure 27: Recidivism Analysis
(Mediation and Matched Comparison Group)

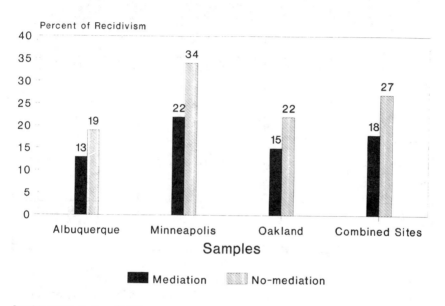

Combined Mediation: N=160
Combined No Mediation N=160

As Figure 27 indicates, juvenile offenders in the three mediation programs committed considerably fewer additional crimes within the one-year period following mediation than did similar offenders in the court-administered restitution program. For the combined sites, the mediation sample had a recidivism rate of 18%, while the no-mediation sample had a much higher rate of 27%. That they also tended to commit crimes that were less serious than the offense for which they were referred to the mediation program is indicated in Table 16. For those offenders in the victim-offender mediation programs who committed subsequent crimes, 41% were involved in less serious crimes, while 12% of those in the matched comparison group who committed subsequent crimes were involved in less serious crimes.

Table 16: Seriousness of Recidivism

	ALBUQUER- QUE		MINNEA- POLIS		OAKLAND		TOTAL	
	Med.	Match	Med.	Match	Med.	Match	Med	Match
Total recidivism	6	9	19	29	4	5	29	43
a. More serious offense	1	5	8	10	2	3	11	18
b. Less serious offense	4	0	6	5	2	0	12	5
c. Same level of seriousness	1	4	5	14	0	2	6	20
Total N	48	48	85	85	27	27	160	160
Recidivism rate	13%	19%	22%	34%	15%	19%	18%	27%

While the victim-offender mediation process appears to have had an effect on suppressing further criminal behavior, this finding is not statistically significant. Even though the difference between the mediation and comparison samples approached significance, and missed by very little, the possibility that this apparent effect occurred by chance cannot be ruled out.

This finding of a marginal but non-significant reduction of recidivism is consistent with two English studies of victim-offender mediation (Dignan, 1990; Marshall and Merry, 1990). Only one study in the U.S. is known (Schneider, 1986) to have found a significant impact of mediation upon offender recidivism. The program in that study, however, did not employ the same type of procedures used by the programs described in the present cross-site analysis of victim-offender mediation. A number of other studies (Butts and Snyder, 1991; Schneider, 1986; Schneider and Schneider, 1984) have found that juvenile offenders involved in a structured restitution program had lower recidivism rates than either offenders with no restitution obligation or offenders in a non-structured, "ad-hoc" restitution program of the court.

It is important to realize that the comparison-group samples in this recidivism analysis consist of a matched sample of offenders who were involved in a structured restitution program. In fact, the largest comparison group was drawn from Hennepin County (Minneapolis area), a highly structured, well-managed and adequately staffed restitution program that has received a considerable amount of national recognition over the years. If the comparison-group samples for this cross-site analysis of victim-offender mediation had consisted of similar offenders who were not in a structured restitution program or who did not even have a restitution obligation, different findings may have emerged. The study would have been more likely to have detected a significant impact of mediation (as a process for implementing restitution) on lowered recidivism.

For some, a finding of a marginal but non-significant impact of the mediation process upon reducing offender recidivism may come as a disappointment. For others, including the author, it comes as no surprise. Rather, such a finding is consistent with recidivism studies related to other community justice alternative programs. It could be argued that it is naive to think that a time-limited intervention such as mediation by itself (perhaps four to eight hours per case) would be likely to have a dramatic effect on altering criminal and delinquent behavior, in which many other factors related to family life, education, chemical abuse and available opportunities for treatment and growth are known to be major contributing factors.

A major limitation of recidivism as an outcome measure is its "all-or-nothing" nature. For example, if an offender in mediation does not recidivate, the program receives credit for this "success." In reality, it is quite possible that the program had little positive impact but that the offender had a supportive family and a group of peers that kept him or her out of trouble. Conversely, if the offender in mediation does commit another crime, the program is saddled with a "failure." The mediation intervention may, however, have been the most positive thing that occurred for the offender in response to his or her criminal behavior, but lack of family support and a gang of friends with criminal tendencies drew the offender back into crime. The point is that criminal and delinquent behavior is far more complex than suggested by such a dichotomous measure as recidivism. Many other things are going on in the life of a juvenile offender than simply the program he or she is involved in. Ideally, it would be preferable to measure the impact of a number of interventions (i.e., family counseling, educational assistance, job training and mediation) on reducing future criminal behavior. Such a measure, although more complex and costly, would be likely to offer a more accurate assessment of how recidivism can be reduced.

We would argue that the most important and realistic criterion related to recidivism and mediation is not the reduction of criminal behavior, as desirable as that is. Rather, the most important criterion is whether offenders in a victim-offender mediation program recidivate at levels no higher than similar offenders in other programs or court interventions. As documented in this report, there are numerous other benefits of the victim-offender mediation process, for both parties. If these benefits occur, with no additional risk of higher rates of criminal behavior, we would argue that, on balance, these programs are quite effective. This is particularly seen in the significant impact of mediation upon successful completion of restitution, and upon reducing the fear and anxiety of crime victims.

9. Mediation Observations: Case Examples and Analysis

- *Case #1: Battery*
- *Case #2: Car theft*
- *Case #3: Burglary*
- *Case #4: Burglary and theft*
- *Dangers and pitfalls*

To better understand how the mediation process actually works, mediation sessions were observed at each of the three primary program sites in Albuquerque, Minneapolis and Oakland. Particularly since so much of the mediation process is based upon verbal and non-verbal communication skills, observing a sample of mediation sessions was critical. A total of 28 observations—14 in Minneapolis, 12 in Albuquerque and 2 in Oakland—were made. Research assistants used an observation protocol to guide them in viewing all mediation sessions.

Four composite observations of mediation sessions will be presented in order to display a range of case examples involved in the mediation process. A qualitative analysis of the observations will then be presented, including a number of dangers and pitfalls. The four examples were constructed through identifying common characteristics among the total number of mediation sessions that were observed. Statements by participants that are presented in these examples are based on the actual mediations that were observed, although they are paraphrased.

COMPOSITE OBSERVATIONS OF MEDIATION SESSIONS

Case Example #1: "In the Yard Again"

The following mediation meeting took place in a pleasant room in a neighborhood church. None of the participants are members of this particular church. The offender, Brian, is a 15-year-old white male charged with battery. The victim, Sarah, is a 14-year old white female. She was struck in the leg by a pellet fired by the offender from his air rifle. The offender is accompanied by his mother; the victim, by her mother and stepfather. Also present is the mediator, John.

The offender is hesitant and avoids making eye contact with anyone. He finally finds a spot on the floor at which to stare. The victim anxiously fiddles with her hands. After the introductions, the mediator explains the ground rules for the meeting, as well as her role as mediator. She invites both sides to be respectful and open to telling their stories. The mediator invites Sarah to begin.

"I was in my own yard working in the garden. I was bent over weeding when I felt a sharp sting in my right leg. Some blood was oozing from my leg." The victim seems to lose concentration and is close to tears.

The mediator elicits more of Sarah's story. "What did you do then?"

"I turned around and saw him and his friend running toward his house. He had a gun in his hand. I thought, 'My God, he shot me!' And I started screaming."

"What happened then?"

The victim's mother responds. "I heard the screams and dashed out of the house to see what was wrong. A little blood was coming from her wound, but she was screaming almost beyond control. I got her into the house where we washed the wound. I felt a tiny hard lump and found the pellet but could not get it out."

"I called the police," chimed in the victim's stepfather, "and we took her to the trauma center at the hospital. Medical staff calmed her down and very simply removed the pellet. We then went home with a still very frightened girl on our hands. It was a helluva thing to happen; we had just moved in the weekend before."

"Brian, why don't you tell us what happened that morning?" asked the mediator.

Without glancing up, Brian responds, "Well, me and my friend were in the backyard shooting around. I didn't really aim at her. I didn't really think the gun could shoot that far."

"You didn't really want to hurt me."

"No, I didn't think we could hit you even if I tried."

"Didn't you hear me yell?"

"Yeah."

"Well, then, why did you run away?'

"We were scared. Real scared. Thought maybe we had really hurt you."

Silence ensues. Victim and offender seem to feel that they have little to add.

The stepfather points out to the offender that things could have been worse. "You could have put out an eye; you could have blinded her."

"I know. I know. That's why we were so scared," the offender moans. "I'm sorry it happened. It was stupid." Both mothers are visibly moved by Brian's comments.

The mediator moves the discussion toward possible restitution. "I am sure that your apology is appreciated, Brian, but how else might you begin to repay Sarah and her family for the pain and suffering that they went through because of you?"

"I don't know."

Turning to Sarah's parents the mediator asks, "How much were the hospital bills?"

"Ah, $750 with a $300 deductible," Sarah's mother replies. "If he could repay the deductible," the victim's stepfather suggests, "we could call it even."

"Can you do that?" asks the mediator. The offender nods. The mediator continues. "With your paper-route job, you could pay $50 a month for six months. Is that OK with you?"

"Yeah, I can do that."

"Is that OK with everyone else?" The mediator looks around as all nod agreement.

As the mediator begins to fill out a contract form, the offender's mother says, "I think that $50 a month is fair, but I don't think it is enough given what we are trying to do here and given the amount of personal trauma that Brian caused Sarah and her family. I think he should have to do something more personal."

The mediator looks at Brian. "Do you have any ideas?"

"He could do my homework for a month," says Sarah with a relaxed smile.

"No, that won't be needed," chuckles Sarah's mother, "but some help with the yard would certainly be appreciated. And we do want to be good neighbors."

As the mediator writes up the contract there is some side discussion. The offender's mother talks about how embarrassing all of this has been and how she has punished Brian. "There is no more air rifle, ever."

All parties sign the contract. The mediator thanks everyone for coming and for being so cooperative. The families go out together, and the last comment heard was that of the offender's mother. "Now maybe I can go out in the yard again and look across the fence."

Case Example #2: "Which Car?"

This mediation took place in a small meeting room at a local community center. The mediator, James, is at the head of the table. Edward, the 15-year old white offender is on the left of James. The offender is slumped in his chair trying to appear at ease. Alice, the 25-year old African-American victim is across from Edward. She appears confident with her hands folded neatly in her lap. Edward, along with other friends, is charged with stealing Alice's car.

The mediator begins: "Before we start I want to go over some ground rules. Each of you will have an opportunity to tell your story of events as you experienced them. I want you to be respectful, listen, and not use abusive language. Express you feelings. We will then try to work out some kind of an agreement. If you cannot come to an agreement, that is OK, but hopefully you will. As you know, I am not on the staff at the court, but any agreement which you make here will be sent to the court. Are there any questions?"

"If there are no questions, who would like to start?"

The offender shrugs.

After a few brief moments, the victim says, "I can start."

"I had a frantic day at the office and stopped at the grocery store so I wouldn't have to go out later. When I got home, I parked at the curb as usual. Normally I lock the car each time I carry a load up to the apartment. Apparently, I forgot. As I was putting away items in the freezer, a friend knocked on the door. She said, 'I heard noises inside but didn't expect to find you here.'

"Why not?" I asked. She said, 'Because of your car. Did someone drive you home?'

I said, 'Of course not, I parked it right out front." She said, 'The hell you did. It ain't out there now.'

'What!' I pushed past my friend to look out the window. I was shocked. It wasn't there. I still don't see how they could have stolen it so quickly. But they did."

The mediator asks, "How did you feel at that time?"

"Shocked. Dumb. Invaded. At a loss of what to do. I thought maybe they would just take the car for a ride and drop it back."

"When did you see the car next?"

"It was about four weeks later when the police called."

"Why don't you tell Edward what you saw when you went down to the garage? Tell him how you felt."

Looking directly across the table at Edward, Alice responds. "It was a damn mess. The trunk lid was gone. The inside was carved up. Hardly any of the upholstery was together. The shifter was missing. Windshield broken. Two tires gone, the other two smashed. I was told many of the parts under the hood were gone; I didn't look. The car was totaled."

"How did you feel when you saw it?" the mediator asks again.

"Helpless. What was I going to do?" Then looking right at Edward, Alice says, "And I thought to myself, what little bastard would do such a thing, and how I would like to get my hands on him. Ripping off my car was one thing—ripping it up was another."

Edward has come to attention. "Which one was it?"

"How many others were there?" Alice asks. "It was the 1985 yellow Subaru."

"Did it have two side mirrors?"

"No."

"Were there clothes in the back?"

"Yeah, there was a clown suit that my little boy had worn to a party the week before."

"OK, I remember your car. It wasn't all that much of a car, but it was unlocked."

"Why would you want my car, anyway?"

Edward responds, "It was something to do. Me and my friends, we were walking by. Someone always checks the cars out as we go. Yours was the first one that was unlocked. We took it for a ride. One of my friends wanted to leave it in the woods where he could go back and lift parts. So we had a party in the car. We had picked up some booze and ate some of the food left in the car. A couple guys got a little wild with their knives. But I don't know about the missing parts. That must have happened later."

"Why did it take so long to find the car?" Alice wants to know.

"I don't know. He must have hid it good in the brush. Or maybe the cops didn't look too hard."

The mediator asks Alice, "How do you feel now?"

"Relieved to be getting this thing done. Still upset that my car was ripped off."

"How do you feel, Edward?" James asks.

"OK. Glad there is no jail."

"Anything else?" asks the mediator. Victim and offender shake their heads. "Then we are ready to see whether you can come to some agreement about restitution. "Alice, what was the extend of your financial loss?"

"Well, the car was totaled. It was valued at $3,000. I had a $500 deductible. The insurance paid $2,500 so I am out $500."

"How much would you like in restitution?"

"Well, I would like to get my $500 back. I think it is only fair. After all, I had to suffer all the hassles besides the loss of the car itself."

"What about you, Edward?" the mediator asks. "What's fair from your point of view?"

"You want to know what I think is fair?"

"Yeah."

Alice is watching Edward intently.

"Sure she deserves her money back," says Edward looking directly at Alice. "That's only fair." He turns and addresses James. "Since there were four of us, can it be split four ways?"

Alice also turns to the mediator. "That's what I was expecting."

"OK. If that's agreeable to each of you, I think that is fine," responds the mediator. "While I begin to draw up the contract, Edward why don't you tell Alice how you will be able to pay her back. She may want to know that you will not have to steal in order to pay her back." Both offender and victim chuckle.

Edward explains, "I work at a place like this. A community center. I do all kinds of jobs. I get paid $4 an hour. I get to keep one dollar; the other three go to you."

"What seems like a reasonable target date, Edward?" the mediator wants to know.

"How about two months. If I put in eight to ten hours a week, that should do it."

"Yeah, that ought to work. Two months from today. Is that OK with you, Alice?"

Alice nods in agreement.

"OK, if you will both look this over and sign at the bottom. I will send this contract to Edward's probation officer."

Both sign the document. "I want to thank each of you for being here and for participating," the mediator concludes.

Edward nods.

Alice comments with a sigh of relief. "I'm just glad it's over."

Case Example #3: "Valued Valuables"

The following mediation occurred in the kitchen of the victim's home at the victim's request. Present were the offender, a 16-year-old white male charged with burglary; the middle-aged, white home owners; and the mediator.

After the participants have gathered around the table with the offender sitting across from the victims, the mediator, Sandy, begins.

"I want to thank each of you for being willing to meet. As I have said to each of you before, I am a trained community volunteer, not employed by the court system. I will, however, report to the court the outcome of this meeting.

As we look back on the events of last July 16, we will begin by considering what each of you experienced that evening, what you felt then and now, and, if possible, we will see if there is some way for Joe to repay you, Mr. and Mrs. Johnson. A restitution contract will be drawn up only if you can agree to something satisfactory. I am not here to impose a contract on you, and I will not do so. Please be open with your feelings. Feel free to ask questions of each other. I do expect you to be civil with one another. My role is to help keep things moving a bit, if need be, and to be a resource for each of you. Are there any questions? If not, who would like to begin?"

"I'll go ahead," replies Mr. Johnson. "We went out to dinner and a movie afterward. We got back here around 11:30 p.m. I knew something was wrong right away. I could sense it. We usually leave that light on over the sink when we go out at night. It wasn't on. I told Vera to wait at the door. My heart was pounding something terrific as I turned on the kitchen lights and then the hall lights. The kitchen was OK. But from the light off the hallway I could see a chair turned over in the living room. I stopped and listened, but didn't hear a thing. Thought about calling the police, but couldn't wait that long. I turned all the lights on I could find. It seemed clear that whoever had been there had left, but they certainly left a mess. That was as terrified as I had been since the war."

As Mr. Johnson pauses, Mrs. Johnson picks up their story. "Once it seemed safe, I followed Paul into the living room. I just sat on the floor and cried. My Peruvian vase lay shattered upon the hearth. That vase had been given to me by my grandmother who had received it from her grandfather who had spent most of his life sailing the great ships. Who would do such a thing? I could better understand it if they had taken it...but to smash it to smithereens just didn't make sense."

Saying this, Mrs. Johnson looks sharply at Joe. "And it still doesn't," her voice shaking. "Why did you do it?" she weeps. "Why did you have to smash it?"

"We didn't know what we were doing," responds Joe in a halting fashion. "We didn't know it would mean so much to anyone...I'm sorry, we didn't know."

Collecting himself, Joe begins to tell of his experience that evening. "Art, Jill and me were riding around. We had picked up a few six packs and had downed most of them when Jill said, 'Let's have some fun! I know a house that's got some of those fancy foreign rugs. They're probably worth a lot. It would be easy to get them.' She had been in the house recently responding to an ad. Well, we found the house, drove by slowly. Nothing was happening. There was a little light coming from the kitchen, but that was it. We got out, walked around the house until we found a bathroom window open. There was no problem getting in. Then we made our way into the living room to see the rugs. There were two of them. Not very big. As I rolled up the rugs, Jill and Art started dancing on the bare floor. I wanted to get out of there, but they kept on making like they were slow dancing to music. They became silly, probably too much booze, and started throwing pillows around. Next thing, Art, grabs the vase and tosses it to Jill and Jill tosses it back, but Art makes no attempt to catch it. It knocks against the fireplace and smashes. It shouldn't have happened. That's not why we were there. I'm sorry, but that's how it was."

Seeing his wife in tears, Mr. Johnson responds. Raising his voice he asks, "Do you do this often—breaking into people's houses to have fun?

"Not often." Joe continues, "No..."

Mr. Johnson interrupts. "How many others have there been?"

"I don't know."

Turning to the mediator, Mr. Johnson says "You didn't tell us we were dealing with an expert."

"Joe hasn't been arrested for burglary before. What he is saying to you is news to me."

"Well, I don't know. How are we supposed to make sense out of something that doesn't make sense in the first place?" grumbles Mr. Johnson.

Mrs. Johnson, looking directly at Joe, asks in a steady, strong voice, "What do you think we should do, young man?"

"I don't know. You got the rugs back already. I can't bring the vase back. What do you want me to do?"

"No, you can't bring the vase back. It's gone. And I can see in your eyes that you share some of our sadness for that. One thing you can do is to help us feel more secure in this house. I haven't had a restful night's sleep since the house was broken into. I want you to show us how to keep burglars out."

"OK, I can do that."

"The girl will pay our insurance deductible on the vase and I want her to do that alone since she broke our trust. We will never place another ad in any paper. But, somehow, you must do more than help make our house secure. You must take pride in something of value to you, of something that you helped create," says Mrs. Johnson reflectively. "I think I have it," she says, looking at her husband. Mrs. Johnson begins to smile. Turning back to Joe, she says "We are redecorating our children's chapel at church. All the work is being done by volunteers. I want you to help. It will be hard, dirty work—scraping, tearing up old carpet and laying down new, and painting. Once completed, there will be something to be proud of. Will you help?"

"How long will this take? When would I do it?"

"I guess no one knows for sure how long it will take. Probably three to four months. Work will be done mainly on Saturdays, with maybe an evening or two now and then. How about four hours a week?"

Joe nods in agreement.

"But you must stay until the chapel is completed. And as far as the others are concerned, you're just a young friend who has agreed to help us. They don't need to know anymore than that. OK."

"OK."

"Is that OK with you, Mr. Johnson?" asks the mediator.

"If it's OK with Vera, it's OK with me. She's always too damned soft-hearted. I guess she's not going to change now. Who knows, it may do him some good. It will at least keep him busy some."

"Good enough. I will begin to write up this agreement in the form of a contract. Is next Saturday OK for the security check and then starting work on the chapel the following Saturday?"

"It's OK with me," says Joe.

"That's good for us," says Mr. Johnson. "Ten o'clock sharp. At the front door. You don't have to come through the window."

As the mediator makes out a contract Mrs. Johnson asks, "Joe, have you been in a chapel much?"

"No, not much."

"He's probably been in other people's houses, uninvited, more often than that," quips Mr. Johnson, eliciting soft laughter from everyone around the table.

The mediator invites each person to sign the document and thanks the Johnsons for allowing the meeting to take place in their home. Everyone rises seemingly not knowing quite what to do. Mr. Johnson finally reaches for Joe's hand and shakes it. "Good luck, kid. You better be on time Saturday morning."

Case Example #4: "Wanted: A Good Time"

Present for the following mediation were David and Maria Sanchez, owners of the Triangle J Grocery and General Store; Frederico Angeles, a 17 year old, who, along with others, is charged with breaking and entering, burglary and theft; and Jane Jenson, mediator. The mediation takes place in the basement of a local church.

Mr. and Mrs. Sanchez arrive first. Maria carries in several folders clearly containing bills, insurance forms and other forms of documentation. David is quite grim. They greet the mediator and are ushered into the mediation room. The mediator's materials are at the head of the table. Mr. and Mrs. Sanchez sit on the side of the table to Jane's left. There is very little casual conversation as they await the arrival of Frederico. The mood is tense.

About ten minutes later, Frederico arrives. He is neat in appearance and smiles quite naturally. He apologizes for being late, saying something about traffic. Frederico sits across from Mr. and Mrs. Sanchez on the mediator's right. He acknowledges the store owners with a nod and a smile. They, in turn, stare directly at Frederico while ignoring his presence.

Jane introduces the participants. Mr. and Mrs. Sanchez continue to disregard Frederico.

Jane begins to explain the mediation process. "On January 20, 1991, Frederico and three of his friends broke into the Sanchez store and stole several items. Today, because of your willingness, as well as the desire of the court, we have come together to discuss what Frederico can do to make amends and for each of you to go on with your lives. We will go back to try to understand what happened on that night. Each of you will have an opportunity to talk about your feelings, then and now. And we will look at the Sanchez's losses and see if Frederico can do anything to replace any of those losses."

"There are some important ground rules that I want to remind you. I want you to talk to each other. I am here to help you talk to one another. I am not here to judge or take sides. However, I will not let things get out of hand. You may express you own feelings as fully as possible. But you will not be allowed to badger or abuse one another. If that were to persist, then this meeting would have to be stopped. While I am not an officer of the court, I am required to write a report describing this meeting and any agreements which may come out of it for the court. The court has responsibility for supervising any agreement reached here. Do any of you have any questions before we begin?" After pausing, the mediator continues. "If there are no questions, who would like to begin by telling us about your experiences the morning of January 20?"

Immediately, Mr. Sanchez says, "Let him start. If it weren't for him and his kind, none of us would have to be here."

Jane turns to Frederico and says, "Would you be willing to begin, Frederico, by telling us what happened that night?"

"Sure," says Frederico as he slouches a bit. "Me and my friends were partying. We ran out of beer. Sammy says, 'Let's go get some beer.' We all got in the car and started driving. It was about 1 a.m. Everything was closed. Sammy says, 'No problem. I know a place we can get into easy.'

"In a few minutes we were in the parking lot behind the 'J.' We all knew the place. Everybody knows the 'J.' We get snacks there and meet people there." With a smile he adds, "The parking lot behind the store is a good place to mess around with girls. Usually you don't get hassled there.

"Anyway, Sammy had noticed before a broken window in the storeroom and knew it would be an easy thing to get into the building. We broke out the remaining jagged glass and climbed through the window. We were only after beer. All we wanted was a good time.

"When we got in, Sammy and I ran to the cooler and picked up several six packs of beer and grabbed some chips and started out of there. But something happened. The two other guys we were with went wild. Rather than getting some beer and going, they started tipping over shelves. They tried to pry open the cash register. That didn't make any sense. I knew there wouldn't be any money in it.

"Sammy and I tried to get them out, but they got real mad because they couldn't find any money. They kept rummaging around tipping things over as they went. They finally found two guns and that seemed to slow them down. We kept telling them that we had to get the hell out of there. We had been there too long. Finally, we left and they followed."

"The way you tell it, sounds like you didn't do a thing," retorts Mr. Sanchez. "I don't believe you at all. You're no angel."

With a shaking voice, Frederico responds. "No, I'm no angel. But I didn't mess up your store either. I stole some beer, I admit that. But I didn't steal any guns and I didn't trash the place—that's kids stuff."

Before her husband could speak again, Maria jumps in. "If you're telling the truth, why didn't you stop the others—they wrecked the place."

"We couldn't. They wouldn't listen until they tired out."

"Were they on anything?" asks Mr. Sanchez.

"Yeah, we had been drinking, and some uppers and stuff were passed around. I don't know how much they had. But they really went wild. I'm sorry about that. I didn't want that to happen."

"You should have thought of that before you broke into the store," said Mr. Sanchez. Frederico nods.

After considerable silence, Jane asks Frederico to explain how he was caught.

"As soon as we got in the car and away from the store we opened the beer. Unfortunately, Sammy ran a stop sign and a cop stopped us. We were taken to detention and later released."

"You didn't tell the police about our store?" asks Mr. Sanchez.

"No. I didn't figure the cops needed any help. We couldn't do much about it by then anyway. Later in the morning two cops came by. The had found out about the store and went to talk to Sammy about it. He cracked, so we all got hauled in again."

"How did you feel when you were arrested?" asks Jane.

"I didn't feel good. I wished we could have got out of there before the place was wrecked. I wished we had just gone home when we ran out of beer. I knew this was going to mean trouble."

"Mr. and Mrs. Sanchez, would either of you or both of you like to tell Frederico what you found that morning as you went to open the store? How did you feel about what you saw?"

"It was a damn mess. I wanted to kill someone," says Mr. Sanchez. "When I saw all the stuff thrown about and broken, I saw all the hours of sweat and tears that we put in the store parade before my eyes. You can't know the emptiness we felt. It looked like mad animals were fighting in our store."

"Why? Why? Why?" Mrs. Sanchez whispers as she quietly sobs.

Frederico appears somewhat shaken by the woman across from him. "It wasn't supposed to happen that way. We'll help make things right, somehow."

"Even if you really wanted to, there's no way you can make things the same. We lost too much." Reaching for the folder, Mr. Sanchez notes, "We lost $9,000 in destroyed inventory, another $5,500 in structural damage to freezers, shelving, light fixtures, cash registers and so on. And you actually stole less than $50 worth of goods, plus the guns valued at $250. That's a total of $14,800. Do you have that kind of money?...I didn't think so," he adds as he sees the shock on Frederico's face.

"How are you operating the store now, Mr. Sanchez?" Jane asks.

"Just barely. The insurance was slow, and then they only paid $3,500 of the structural damage and $2,000 of the inventory loss. The guns were returned. We have rebuilt some of the shelving, but we cannot afford to replace all the inventory. We still owe bills on much of the destroyed inventory besides trying to replace it with something we can sell." Shaking his head Mr. Sanchez adds, " I don't know. We may not survive."

Frederico has been listening without his usual smile. Jane turns to him and says, "What do you think? Is there anything you can do to help these people recover their losses?"

"Get off it!" snaps Mr. Sanchez. "You are as responsible as anybody else. You went along with the break-in and stealing the beer. Things just got out of control. You might want to choose your friends better in the future. But now what are you going to do?"

"We came here thinking that you would want to help undo a wrong," interjects Mrs. Sanchez. "You look like a young man who wants to have fun, but you don't look like a bad man. It was important for me to see you. Now I remember you from before. You have been in our store many times. Why don't you help us? That store is our whole life and we may lose it."

"What can I do? I'm no magician."

While everyone seems at the point of throwing up their hands, Jane intercedes. "Well, let's look at this problem a little piece at a time. The two who caused most of the damage have admitted to it and are in jail. Sammy and Frederico have this opportunity to work out something else. It would probably take years for them to raise $9,000, which would probably be too late for you. Are there other ways which they can help, particularly Frederico? Is there anything you need besides money?"

Mr. Sanchez responds by saying, "We could certainly use some labor. There is a lot of shelving and storage bins to be rebuilt yet. And we could use help with stocking because we had to lay off two of our three employees. We couldn't afford to keep them in the face of our losses. Maybe we could get some help."

"We could sure use the help." Mrs. Sanchez interjects. "My husband is putting in too many hours. It's not good for him."

"How much did you pay the employees who were laid off?" Jane asks.

"$5 per hour," says Mr. Sanchez.

Jane looks at Frederico and asks, "Frederico, do you have any ideas?"

"Yeah, I could work for them part time, but I already have a part-time job."

"What hours do you work?"

"Three to seven in the evening, five days a week."

"Could you work mornings or Saturdays?"

"Yeah."

"Would that be helpful, Mr. Sanchez?"

"Sure, but how do we know we can trust him?"

"If I screw this up I go to jail; I'm not going to jail," says Frederico with commitment.

"OK." Mr. Sanchez replies.

Jane begins to pull things together. "For Frederico to pay off his share of the outstanding portion of $9,000, a sum of $2,250, he would need to work for you 22 weeks, or about six months at 20 hours a week at $5 per hour."

"That's a long time," gasps Frederico. "What if I could get a full-time job three months from now? Could I pay the rest of it off?"

Mr. Sanchez shrugs and says, "Sounds alright to me. We just want to get paid back. If he can get a better job and pay us back quicker, all the better."

"Very good. I'll write this up in a contract." Jane adds, "I appreciate everyone being willing to hang in there until you could come up with a workable agreement."

After some moments of silence and small talk while Jane writes up the contract, Jane presents the contract to them identifying the various points agreed to.

Mr. Sanchez, looking at Frederico asks, "When can you begin?"

"How about next Monday morning?"

"That'll be OK. Be at the store at 8 a.m. and I'll get you started. I think you know where the store is."

"Yeah," Frederico smiles.

The participants stand and thank Jane, who shakes hands with each of them.

A QUALITATIVE LOOK AT VICTIM-OFFENDER MEDIATION: DANGERS AND PITFALLS

Detailed observations of actual victim-offender mediation cases reveal, for the most part, what one would expect given the rhetoric of victim-of-fender mediation and training materials. One can readily see the move-ment through the stages of mediation from introductions, to discussion of facts surrounding the events, to discussion of feelings and getting questions answered, to identifying losses and negotiating restitution contracts, to bringing closure to the mediation session itself.

The composite observation cases provide an opportunity to see and experience the mediation process. The reader will look at these cases and think, "Why didn't the mediator do this or that?" Certainly, different mediators would have varied in their handling of the cases, which are not meant to be pristine, "this-is-the-way-to-do-it" examples. We hope that they closely approximate real-life cases, where the ideal is seldom attain-able. Also, individual mediator variation is to be anticipated to a certain extent. Even though these victim-offender mediation programs are sup-ported by fairly extensive training and supervision, there is neither an expectation nor a desire to simply create mediator clones.

Although the patterns we see through the observations generally mirror expectations as presented through training, acceptable variations reflecting the personalities of individual mediators is evident. It is apparent that some dangers loom that threaten the process of victim-offender mediation.

The Presence of Parents

More and more it seems that we are seeing parents involved in mediation, regardless of whether the child is the victim or the offender.

That parents have the right to be present seems clear; that they can have a positive influence is also clear.

The presence of parents, however, can pose some tricky situations for mediators. Key to personalizing and humanizing an approach to justice is that the offender take responsibility for his or her actions. Parents can, at times, plead with a child not to say "I did it, " or may attempt to bully the child into saying "I did it" to help teach him or her a lesson. Parents can be very helpful in supporting their child, while allowing the child to be responsible. They can help clarify situations, make useful suggestions for alternative restitution plans and demonstrate their continuing care. Parents can also appear to be simply buying off the victim by saying, "Just tell us what you want and we'll write you a check. We don't want any more hassles."

Perhaps more attention should be placed on helping parents be present while empowering their youngsters to take responsibility. When the mediator meets with parents before the mediation session, considerable emphasis could be placed on discussing constructive roles for parents. Just as in other elements of training, one can role-play how to regain some sense of balance after a parent has made a bold effort to take control of the process. For example,

Victim's father: "I think this little shit should pay $500—twice the value of the bike he stole. After all, we're keeping him out of jail."

Mediator: "Mr. Jones, we appreciate you and your daughter, Amanda, being willing to participate. But, as I said earlier, we will not tolerate verbally abusing either the victim or the offender. And I cannot sit here and let you get twice the value of the stolen bike; the court would not go along with that anyway. Andy (offender), do you want to continue trying to reach an agreement?"

Offender: "Yeah."

Mediator: "Amanda, do you want to try to reach an agreement?"

Victim: "Yes."

Mediator: "Mr. Jones, do we have your assurance that you will not again attempt to verbally abuse Andy so that we can come to an agreement that seems fair to everyone? If not, we will have to conclude that no agreement can be reached."

In this situation, the mediator clearly takes control to cool things down but then gives control back to the participants, beginning with the offender, to see if continuing this is desirable. By reestablishing the groundrules, the mediator is also reestablishing the balance of power within the setting. This is an important factor to keep in mind: We do not want the victim-offender process to be one in which the victim is re-victimized or the offender is victimized.

A major benefit of having parents present is the opportunity for all involved to discover that parents of the victim and parents of the offender are often victims themselves. The composite observation, "In the Yard Again," demonstrates this well as the mother of the victim leaves the mediation exclaiming "Now maybe I can go out in the yard again and look across the fence."

Co-Mediators: Who's In Charge?

Numerous situations arise where a co-mediator brings needed additional resources to a meeting. Co-mediation is sometimes used to achieve gender, ethnic or racial balance with the offender and victim. It may also be used as an equalizer in cases where the number of offenders and/or victims present for mediation can be overwhelming. Finally, co-mediation is sometimes desirable if the nature of the offense is particularly sensitive and complex.

The presence of more than one mediator also creates its own set of dangers. There may be no apparent agreement on strategy in a particular mediation. Mediators may be played off against each other to the point that mediation is needed to settle their differences. Confusion as to who is in charge poses a problem for the participants. This confusion can be an advantage as it may be more difficult to form an alliance with both mediators. Such confusion can be a real disadvantage if a participant does not know who to rely on or cannot establish trust. Taking risks in a safe environment is difficult enough; taking risks in an uncertain environment may not be worth doing.

To avoid confusion—and without making an issue of it—the mediators need to decide who is taking the lead, and who will help facilitate and clarify. If the mediators are clear then the participants will likely be clear without being told. With such clarity, attempts at playing one mediator off against the other are greatly minimized, and confusion is reduced for everyone.

Using Silence or Who Will Blink First?

Too often observers note, "If only he could trust silence." "Mediator fills dead time with the sound of her voice." "Because of mediator talking too much, no one has time to think."

While many mediators use silence effectively, being comfortable with silence and using it to advance the mediation process remains a problem for others. As suggested above, some folks need time to think out responses and to think through options. Often new information is provided if the mediator is willing to move at a slower pace. Silence provides a kind of structured stress, encouraging participants to take responsibility for the mediation. It fails to be an effective tool, however, if the mediator is the one consistently succumbing to the structured stress of silence. Silence doesn't necessarily mean no one has anything to say; it may simply mean that no one is ready to say anything yet.

Use of silence, perhaps, should be stressed more in training and supervision. Both the "why" (silence can be important to the process) and the "how" (waiting long enough without letting silence kill the process entirely) can be realized. Role-plays could be developed to teach this skill, audiotapes and videotapes of others doing mediation could be critiqued, and audiotapes and videotapes of the trainee doing mediation could be reviewed in this training process. Until the mediator can use silence effectively, the mediator will too often lose control of the mediation process and be too easily manipulated by a shrewd offender or victim.

Lost Opportunities

There is a disturbing quality, at times, in the observation of a deadly kind of routinization beginning in some cases to set in during the mediation process. There is a sort of methodical, mechanical tone about the process. The nub of this quality seems to be expectations regarding restitution. It appears that for some, restitution is the name of this game. "Let's hurry through this feeling stuff and get to the real question, 'How much money am I going to get back?'" Restitution is not an unimportant question, yet is not the only important question for victim-offender mediation.

More disturbing than the single focus of restitution for either victim or offender is the single focus of restitution for the mediator. For some, there seems to be a rush to get to this part of the mediation. It typically may be easier to handle and less potentially volatile. This may be the area in which there are more intangible rewards of gratitude for the mediator. On several occasions, mediators either did not hear or chose to ignore suggestions of non-monetary restitution. The composite cases, "Valued Valuable" and "In the Yard Again," contain suggestions by the victim and offender's mother, respectively, which, although not identical to real-life cases, were similar. In the real-life cases, the suggestions were ignored.

Perhaps, for some, the focus on a "dollar figure both parties can live with" has made it difficult to see and hear alternatives or additional ways in which restitution can be packaged. Being open to creative opportunities offers much for humanizing and personalizing the justice process. Doing yard work, painting a community center or working as a cross-walk attendant are also ways of "paying back," and "making right" that encourage the offender and the victim to see each other as real people in the making and resolving of conflict or crime.

* * *

We have identified four areas of potential danger and pitfalls for the victim-offender mediation process that are apparent from observations of actual cases. While the bulk of the mediations seem to fit the expected patterns and outcomes, there is reason to be concerned about the dangers discussed above. If unchecked, these dangers could over time require yet a new reform—a new program scheme—to humanize and personalize the mediation process.

NOTE: This chapter was written by Robert B. Coates, Ph.D., who served as the senior research associate for the study. Dr. Coates is the Senior Pastor of the First Congregational Church in Salt Lake City, UT. He is a private consultant with an extensive amount of practice and research experience, as well as numerous publications, in the field of juvenile justice, having formerly served on the faculty of Harvard University, the University of Chicago and the University of Utah.

10. Issues to be Faced in Starting a Local Program

- *Goal clarification*
- *Community support*
- *Funding*
- *Target population*
- *Program design*
- *Management information system*
- *Training of mediators*

A number of important tasks that were critical to the initiation and development of an effective program were successfully completed by each of the four victim-offender mediation programs examined in this study. Other programs in the field have faced similar tasks that have focused on the issues of: goal clarification; community/system support; funding; target population; referral source(s); program design; management information systems; and training of mediators.

As the field of victim-offender mediation continues to expand in North America and Europe, it will be important for local program organizers and advocates to address these key issues that are critical to effective program replication.

GOAL CLARIFICATION

The victim-offender mediation process offers a variety of potential benefits. Victims can become directly involved in the justice process. They can let the offender know of the impact that the crime has had on their life and can receive answers to any lingering questions. Victims can directly influence the manner in which the offender is held accountable, through negotiation of a mutually acceptable restitution agreement.

Through mediation, offenders are allowed to be held accountable in a very personal fashion. Offenders have the opportunity to repair the damage they are responsible for, accept responsibility for their behavior and portray a more human dimension to their character. The opportunity for offering a direct apology to the person they victimized is provided. Offenders who participate in mediation may also avoid a harsher penalty.

The community-at-large also benefits from the increased practice of nonviolent conflict resolution skills that occurs through the presence of a local victim-offender mediation program. Many offenders who participate in a mediation session with their victim are less likely to commit additional crimes. Through diversion of certain cases from the court system to mediation, scarce tax dollars can also be saved.

Precisely because the mediation process has clear benefits for both the offender and the victim, as well as the larger community, it is important for local program organizers to be clear about their goal(s). By definition, the mediation process is grounded in the primary goal of providing a conflict resolution process that is perceived as fair to both the victim and offender. Each local program, however, needs to identify which secondary goals are important for their community.

There are a number of possible secondary goals of the victim-offender mediation process. For example, is the program concerned about crime prevention, offender rehabilitation, victim assistance, community conflict resolution, victim empowerment, victim-offender reconciliation, or serving as an alternative to incarceration? Each of these possible secondary goals are certainly not mutually exclusive. Effective program development, however, will be difficult without local organizers first clarifying which goals are the most important for their specific jurisdiction.

COMMUNITY SUPPORT

The development of community and criminal justice system support for a local victim-offender mediation program is critical. A broad base of support will be required to initiate a new program, particularly because of the predictable initial skepticism regarding the concept of allowing crime victims to meet with the person who victimized them.

One of the first tasks that local program advocates and organizers should complete is a thorough analysis of key local actors within the community and justice system. Key actors might include: judges; prosecutors; defense attorneys; correctional staff; victim advocates; probation staff; directors of victim service agencies; city or county political leaders; clergy people; neighborhood leaders; and civic and corporate leaders. All possible stakeholders in the development of a local victim-offender mediation program should be considered.

The analysis of these key actors should focus upon assessing the degree to which each individual could either offer resistance or significantly influence the development of a new program. It might be helpful to develop a chart in which the names of the key actors, and their position, are listed along the left hand margin and the following four columns are to be filled out for each person. (See Appendix 5: Stakeholder Analysis Form.)

(1) Evaluate their influence/power.

(2) Evaluate their probable support or non-support.

(3) Identify who can influence them.

(4) Develop a strategy to either gain their support or neutralize their active opposition.

Building local support for a new victim-offender mediation program will also require the development of a plan for presenting the concept and program to the public in a clear and understandable fashion, what some would call a marketing strategy. Development of such a plan should include the ability to:

(1) State the purpose of your program in one sentence.

(2) State the human interest aspect of your program in one sentence.

(3) State the public policy/criminal justice system relevance of your program in one sentence.

(4) State briefly the benefits of your program.

(5) Identify briefly any possible self-interest the following key actors might have in your program: judge, prosecutor, defense attorney, probation officer, police or local politicians.

(6) Based on the above, develop a general presentation outline for presenting your program to local officials and the public.

(7) Identify a strategy for utilizing newspapers, radio stations and television stations.

Effective development of a broad base of community support requires preparation of a clear and brief presentation about the program, scheduling many presentations before a wide range of community organizations and justice system agencies, and inviting the active involvement of key actors and others in the actual process of developing and managing the new victim-offender mediation program. Additional strategies for developing support are addressed in the next chapter.

FUNDING

Securing sufficient funds to support the operation of a new victim-offender mediation program is one of the most difficult tasks to be faced during the initial program development process. Fortunately, such mediation programs do not require huge budgets.

The annual expenses (1991 figures) for three of the programs described in this report were: Albuquerque, $31,530; Minneapolis, $123,366; Oakland, $127,176. The Albuquerque program budget is actually more representative of many of the programs operated by small non-profit community agencies, some of which have even smaller budgets in the range of $5,000 to $10,000 (Fagan and Gehm, 1993). With such a small budget, these programs would obviously have to rely very heavily on the use of volunteers. The larger budgets in the Minneapolis and Oakland programs represent more mature and well-developed programs that have expanded considerably. Even these two programs, however, had a much smaller amount of funding ($20,000 to $30,000) during their initial years of development.

Based on a review of 123 victim-offender mediation programs in the U.S., the typical program was found to have a budget of $47,500, with just under three staff persons, 16 volunteer mediators and an annual caseload of 200 referrals (Fagan and Gehm, 1993). The actual size of program budgets is a function of several important variables: caseload projection; use of volunteer mediators; level of existing administrative support; fund raising ability; and public relations responsibilities.

Many programs have begun with relatively small amounts of money, often from private foundations and churches, and later have secured larger amounts of public funding as the program develops. While a small amount of federal funds is available to support victim-offender mediation and reconciliation programs, the most likely source of funding is to be found within the state and, particularly, local private and public sources. The task of securing local funds should not be postponed until all plans for the new program are finalized. Rather, potential funding sources should be identified and researched during the initial planning phase. When the initial plans for the new program are worked out, including a tentative budget, it is often helpful to develop a brief concept paper that can be distributed to potential funding sources. A more thorough proposal will eventually need to be prepared.

A strategy of developing a multiple-source funding base is often helpful. Having several different sources provide funding for a program can often be more effective than a single-source funding base, in which the entire project is dependent upon one grant. If that single grant is lost, the existence of the entire project is immediately threatened. Public agencies, such as probation departments, are in a position to even consider reassigning responsibilities and resources so that only a marginal amount of additional funding may be required. On the other hand, departments that are overburdened with high and growing caseloads will certainly not be in a position to develop a new victim-offender mediation program without a significant amount of new resources.

TARGET POPULATION

In the planning of a new victim-offender mediation program, it is important to identify the target population for case referrals. Will the program focus on juvenile or adult court cases? Will it accept any referrals, regardless of age or type of offense? Will it focus upon only the most minor property offenses, or, will it attempt to receive referrals of more serious property offenses and some violent offenses? These are important questions to address early in the life of the planning process. Depending on the choices made, the program can quickly become stigmatized as another so-called alternative for lightweight cases, many of which would have been essentially ignored by the system, or as an important new effort to deal with more serious offenses.

Within the field of victim-offender mediation and reconciliation, there exist two schools of thought on this important issue. Many would argue that since the primary goal of the mediation process is to resolve the conflict between the victim and the offender, nearly any case referred is appropriate. From this perspective, there is little concern about the seriousness of the offenses, age or circumstances of the offender, or about the possible impact of mediation on the larger justice system (i.e., widening the net of social control versus serving as an actual alternative to court, or even incarceration). Many programs that embrace such a broad definition of their target population tend to receive a high volume of very minor misdemeanor offenses (i.e., lightweight cases).

Others in the field would argue that given the limited resources available to all programs and the relative needs facing individual victims and offenders, as well as the justice system, a more serious range of case referrals should be identified. It is less likely that the program would be marginalized if it worked with more serious cases. The impact of the mediation program in truly diverting certain cases from the justice system or from a penalty of costly incarceration would likely be greater. Victims and offenders involved in more serious cases usually have greater emotional and material needs that could be resolved through mediation.

While working with any case seems logical—if not desirable—in the abstract, it is simply not possible. Many would argue that focusing primarily upon the least serious offenses results in a tremendous under-utilization of the full power and potential of the mediation intervention to create a greater sense of closure and reconciliation among the involved parties. Moreover, it has become increasingly clear that mediation can be very effective in working with cases involving severe trauma and loss, including attempted homicides and homicides (Umbreit, 1989b). The number of such cases remains small, but it is continuing to expand. The mediation process in such cases also requires a number of modifications, advanced training for the mediator and a far more intense case-management process. The fact the mediation can be effective in such severely violent offenses bodes well for the targeting of more serious offenses and the need to limit the negative effects of increased social control through "net widening" (i.e., placing more, not fewer, offenders under the control and influence of the justice system) and "net strengthening" (i.e., providing mediation as an add-on to existing sanctions—usually involving more cost—rather than as a substitute for an existing sanction).

Identifying an appropriate target population for case referrals ulti-mately involves a balance between the desires of the program advocates and the willingness of the criminal justice system to support the new program and experiment by taking some risks. A negotiated process is required between representatives of the referral sources and program staff. Keeping the expressed goals of the program in the forefront of such negotiations is critical. Without such focus, it will become far too easy for the new program to be seduced into taking cases that have little relation-ship to the ultimate goals of the program.

Identifying an appropriate target population also requires open recog-nition of the tremendous resilience of the criminal justice system in coopting true reforms. Many "diversion" programs and "alternatives" that were developed over the past two decades were found to have little real impact in either truly diverting cases from the courts or reducing the use of incarceration. The good intentions of reformers did not often lead to the desired changes. The more local organizers are committed to avoiding the creation of "wider and stronger nets of social control" (Austin and Krisberg, 1981), through not repeating the errors of the past, the more difficult the task of identifying an appropriate target population will be.

PROGRAM DESIGN

The most crucial, yet difficult, task of initiating a new victim-offender mediation program is the need to design the local program in such a way that it will maximize the achievement of its primary goal, with direct impact on the desired target population. Clarification of goals and identification of a target population can easily become an abstract and irrelevant exercise if they are not directly formulated as clear strategies for how a local program will actually operate. For this reason, the task of effective program design is the most demanding and critical step in any local replication effort. Experience in the field of victim-offender mediation has taught that many local organizers underestimate the importance of program design and are often too quick to initiate training of mediators.

While there is certainly no simple or perfect way of designing a local victim-offender mediation program, there are a number of key issues that need to be addressed. These include: program sponsorship; staffing; use of volunteers; point of referral in system; referral criteria and procedures; and use of co-mediators.

Program Sponsorship

Identifying the appropriate agency to sponsor a new victim-offender mediation is extremely important. Agencies that are already identified as strong advocates for either victims or offenders are unlikely to be able to offer a mediation service that requires the use of neutral, impartial third parties. In some communities, the establishment of an entirely new non-profit organization may be appropriate. In other communities, a collaborative effort between a local probation department and a victim services agency may be selected. The victim-offender mediation programs in Albuquerque and Austin are particularly good examples of collaborative efforts between private and public agencies. In Albuquerque, the juvenile probation department and the New Mexico Center for Dispute Resolution sponsor the program. In Austin, the juvenile probation department directly sponsors the program but relies on the local dispute resolution center to provide the volunteer mediators to handle cases.

Staffing

The number of staff required to manage a new victim-offender mediation program can vary a great deal based on the nature of the organization sponsoring the program, the level of new funding secured and the projected caseload. In existing well-established, non-profit community agencies or in some probation departments, it may be possible to initiate a program with a very limited number of staff members. Some programs have begun with essentially a half-time staff person and a pool of volunteers; having at least one and one-half full-time equivalent staff members to initiate the program and coordinate volunteers is far more desirable. Others programs that are not able to receive supportive services from a larger organization (including free office space, telephone, secretarial support, etc.) are likely to need more staff. As programs expand over time, more staff will be required to effectively manage the program.

Use of Volunteers

The use of trained community volunteers needs to be addressed early in the planning process since it has a direct impact on the budget and staff required to initiate the program. The benefits of using volunteers include increased citizen participation in the justice process, broader community exposure to nonviolent conflict resolution skills and reduced costs for the program. Further, volunteers often add a level of enthusiasm and commitment to a program that is a valuable asset.

However, using volunteers in a new mediation program requires a good deal of planning and effort in recruitment, training, and monitoring. Periodic in-service training is important, along with various events to provide recognition and support. The benefits must be examined in the context of the energy and resources that must be expended. Most victim-offender mediation programs have chosen to use community volunteers as mediators.

Point of Referral

The point at which cases are referred to mediation by the justice system is a critical strategic issue to consider. There are at least four possible referral points: directly from the police before a formal charge is filed; after the police have filed a report but prior to a trial, as a diversion from prosecution; after an admission or finding of guilt, but prior to the sentencing or disposition hearing; and after the sentencing hearing. Some programs would accept referrals at any of the above points.

There are benefits and limitations related to using any of these referral points. While mediation is more likely to be an alternative to the court process if cases are received at a pretrial level, it is also more likely that only relatively minor offenses will be referred. If more serious cases, including some violent offenses, are meant to be referred to mediation, it is more likely that the point of referral would be post-conviction or post-adjudication. Some programs find it desirable to have cases referred after an admission of guilt but prior to sentencing. This allows victims to have direct input into the penalty required of their offender and represents a time of high motivation for the offender to make amends.

Referral Criteria and Procedures

The importance of developing clear referral criteria and effective referral procedures cannot be overstated. Failure to address these issues will likely result in few referrals as well as inappropriate cases, both of which can marginalize the program. The experience of many programs shows that clear referral criteria *and* very proactive referral procedures are the most effective. Rather than providing the referral source with a list of criteria and then waiting for referrals to be made, having program staff directly review and select cases at the offices of the referral source is far more effective. An example of clear and concise criteria and procedures would be:

Referral Criteria
- Adult felony offenders convicted of burglary or theft, regardless of prior offenses
- Identifiable loss by victim and need for restitution
- Absence of intense hostility that could lead to violence
- Admission by the offender of complicity in the offense

Referral/Case Management Procedures
- Immediately following conviction, probation staff temporarily place all burglary and theft case files in the VOMP in-basket at the probation office

- Program staff visit the probation office daily to review all burglary and theft cases within 24 hours of conviction
- Program staff select appropriate cases to be referred to mediation, subject to final review by probation staff
- Program staff transfer case information from the file to the VOMP case referral form

The above abbreviated criteria and procedures are offered to emphasize the need for clarity. Actual referral criteria and procedures are likely to be more detailed. Time frames for completing certain procedures can be helpful if they are understood as targets and not rigid goals.

Use of Co-Mediators

In designing the program and preparing for mediation of cases, it will be important to determine if single mediators or co-mediators will be used. There are advantages to both. On the one hand, it is easier to schedule actual mediation sessions when single mediators are used, and a smaller pool of volunteers is required. On the other hand, co-mediators can: increase quality control through peer support and critiquing; provide additional support and help to mediators during the mediation session and through de-briefing after it ends; allow for more flexibility in addressing cross-cultural issues that may be present in the conflict (assuming one of the co-mediators is from the minority culture); and promote broader citizen/volunteer involvement in mediation. Co-mediation can involve having one person serve as the lead mediator, with the other in a secondary role of helping clarify issues or assisting with difficult issues that may arise. It can also involve having the mediators both take the lead in different parts of the session. For example, one mediator could handle the initial opening of the session, and the discussion of the facts and feelings related to the case. The other mediator could then take the lead in reviewing the losses and helping the parties negotiate a mutually acceptable restitution agreement.

MANAGEMENT INFORMATION SYSTEM

The development of a management information system in the planning of a new victim-offender mediation program can provide an effective mechanism for the collecting, storing and retrieving of important information. Management information systems have several uses. These include:

(1) assisting in the delivery of mediation services,

(2) documenting accurately what is done,

(3) facilitating supervision of staff and volunteers,

(4) providing a basis for program evaluation that can inform planning, program development, and policy formulation, and

(5) providing a basis for presenting the program to potential users, funders, and other interested groups.

The concept of a management information system may immediately suggest an endless amount of paperwork and hassle. A good system should, however, actually increase efficiency, streamline paperwork, and systematically provide helpful information to both supervisors and line staff. In order to develop a management information system, the program staff need to determine: what data is needed in order to meet the desired uses of the system; how and in what form the data will be collected; how the data will be managed; and how the system can be used for evaluation, feedback, and reporting purposes.

An example of sample forms used in the management information system of many victim-offender mediation programs includes the following items:

(1) VOMP case record form

(2) VOMP case referral form

(3) letter to victim

(4) letter to offender

(5) mediator narrative report form

(6) progress report form

(7) agreement form

(8) case referral input log

(9) case referral output log

(10) monthly statistical summary form

Some programs have streamlined the number of forms used, while others might have additional forms. A growing number of programs are using computer software for their management information system in order to significantly reduce the volume of paperwork.

TRAINING OF MEDIATORS

A final issue that needs to be addressed as local communities replicate the victim offender-mediation model is that of recruiting and training volunteer mediators. A number of basic characteristics are important to keep in mind as individuals are considered to serve as mediators. These include: good communication skills, particularly reflective listening and assertion; problem solving and negotiation skills; ability to exercise appropriate leadership; good organizational skills; commitment to the philosophy and techniques of nonviolent conflict resolution; and the ability to understand and work within the criminal justice system.

The length of mediation training provided in the victim-offender mediation field can vary from 12 to 40 hours. Training should introduce volunteers to the victim-offender mediation and reconciliation concept, how it operates within the local justice system, and the procedures of the local program. A major portion of the training should focus on communication skills, problem solving and negotiation, and conducting the various elements of the process, including calling the victim/offender, meeting with the victim/offender separately, and then conducting the joint mediation session. Maximum time should be allowed for small group practice of skills and processing. A special unit in all training should focus on the victimization experience, perhaps having a representative from a local victim advocacy program as the presenter. Another unit in training should address the criminal justice process, terminology, and impact on offenders. A probation officer can often be used for this segment of the training. New programs do not have to "reinvent the wheel" of mediation training. A number of excellent training curriculums and video tapes are available, as noted at the end of this chapter.

The ideas presented in this chapter represent only a brief overview of several important issues that need to be addressed as other communities attempt to replicate the victim-offender mediation program model in their jurisdiction. More extensive program development material related to program design, organizing strategies, training of volunteer mediators, and sample forms and procedures is available in *The VORP Book*. This text, along with other written and video resources, is available from:

The PACT Institute of Justice
254 S. Morgan Blvd.,
Valparaiso, IN 46383
(219) 462-1127

A victim-offender training manual and videotape is available from:

Fraser Region Community Justice Initiatives Association
101 - 20678 Eastleigh Crescent
Langley, British Columbia V3A 4C4 CAN
(604) 534-5515

Two mediation training videotapes, one of which models the entire victim-offender mediation process from phone calls to separate meetings to mediation, are available from:

The Center for Creative Justice
304 Lynn Ave.
Ames, IA 50010
(515) 292-3820

A six-minute videotape that provides an overview of the victim-offender mediation process and impact is available from:

Citizens Council Mediation Services
822 South Third Street
Minneapolis, MN 55415
(612) 340-5432

11. Conclusions and Implications

- *Study conclusions*
- *Policy implications*
- *Program implications*
- *Lingering critical issues*
- *Present opportunities*

The study presented in this book represents the largest evaluation of the victim-offender mediation process in North America. A total of 1,153 interviews with crime victims and juvenile offenders in four states, extensive review of program and court records, interviews with court officials and program staff, and observation of 28 mediation sessions resulted in a huge amount of quantitative and qualitative data. While this cross-site analysis of juvenile victim-offender mediation programs offers a number of important conclusions and implications, it also contains a number of limitations.

The necessity of using a quasi-experimental design, without random assignment of subjects into experimental and control groups, eliminates the ability to broadly generalize conclusions to all victims and offenders in the four programs or in similar mediation programs. Early in the study it became evident that the time at which the pre-mediation interviews were conducted, after a separate meeting between the mediator and the subject, was too far into the overall case management process. This resulted in considerably less change between the pre- and post-mediation measurements than initially anticipated, and appears to be related to the fact that at the point of the pre-mediation interview subjects had already agreed to mediation and their expectations were quite high. No acceptable earlier point of administering the pre-mediation interview could be determined without significantly contaminating the normal case management process.

CONCLUSIONS

Several important conclusions that emerged from analysis of the data sources in the study are identified below. While caution must be exercised in generalizing these conclusions to other subjects or programs, they do provide important insight into this growing international field of justice reform.

(1) Victim-offender mediation results in very high levels of client satisfaction (victims, 79%; offenders, 87%) and perceptions of fairness (victims, 83%; offenders, 89%) with the mediation process. This is consistent with a number of previous studies (Coates and Gehm, 1985,1989; Dignan, 1990; Marshall and Merry, 1990; Umbreit, 1988, 1990, 1991c).

(2) The importance among victims and offenders of meeting each other and interacting through the mediation process is documented quantitatively in this study, whereas prior research (Coates and Gehm, 1985, 1989) provided qualitative data related to this issue.

(3) The mediation process has a strong effect on humanizing the justice system response to crime, for both victims and juvenile offenders. This is consistent with the findings of prior studies (Coates and Gehm, 1985, 1989; Marshall and Merry, 1990; Umbreit, 1991c).

(4) The process of victim-offender mediation has a more significant differential effect upon crime victims than offenders (when examining comparison groups), even though both victims and offenders indicate very high levels of satisfaction and perceptions of fairness with mediation.

(5) Victim-offender mediation makes a significant contribution to reducing fear and anxiety among crime victims. Prior to mediation, nearly 25% of victims were afraid of being victimized again by the same offender. After mediation, only 10% were afraid of being revictimized.

(6) Juvenile offenders seem to perceive victim-offender mediation as an equally demanding response to their criminal behavior than other options available to the court. The use of mediation is consistent with the concern to hold young offenders accountable for their criminal behavior (Bazemore, 1990, 1992; Schneider, 1985; Schneider and Schram, 1986).

(7) The specific location and sponsorship of the program had no major impact upon the high degree of client satisfaction and perceptions of fairness with the mediation process, for either victims or offenders.

(8) Victim-offender mediation has strong support from court officials— both judges and probation staff—and is increasingly becoming institutionalized into the juvenile court system.

(9) Mediation is perceived to be voluntary by the vast majority of juvenile offenders who participated in it. Programs in this study appear to have done a better job of presenting mediation as a

voluntary choice to the offender (81% of offenders) than indicated in prior research (Coates and Gehm, 1985, 1989).

(10) Mediation is perceived to be voluntary by the vast majority of victims who participated in it. Although 93% of victims felt they voluntarily chose to participate in mediation, a small number of victims (7%) felt that they were coerced into participating in the program. Whether this perception of coercion was a function of the program staff, mediators, court-related officials or even parents (of juvenile victims) is unclear.

(11) Considerably fewer and less-serious additional crimes were committed within a one-year period by juvenile offenders in victim-offender mediation programs, when compared to similar offenders who did not participate in mediation. Consistent with two recent English studies (Marshall and Merry, 1990; Dignan, 1990), this important finding, however, is not statistically significant because of the size of program samples.

(12) Victim-offender mediation has a significant impact on the likelihood of offenders successfully completing their restitution obligation to the victim (81%), when compared to similar offenders who completed their restitution in a court-administered program without mediation (58%).

(13) There is a small, but important, amount of data from this study suggesting that there is a danger of the mediation process becoming too routine, in such a way that it too could be experienced by some as dehumanizing.

(14) As the field of victim-offender mediation expands and becomes more institutionalized, a danger exists that it will alter its model to accommodate the dominant system of retributive justice, rather than influencing the present system to alter its model to incorporate the more restorative vision of justice upon which mediation is based.

IMPLICATIONS

The following implications for justice policy and direct practice are offered, based upon the study conclusions.

Policy Implications

° Wider public policy consideration should be given to increasing the availability of victim-offender mediation services, perhaps even as a basic right for those victims of crime who would find it helpful.

assuming the offender agrees to such a meeting and a credible mediation program is available to both parties.

- Victim-offender mediation should be more consistently integrated into the large national network of court-sponsored restitution programs, in collaboration with local community-based mediation programs. There is strong evidence that victims of crime are more likely to actually be compensated if the restitution plan is negotiated by the offender and victim.
- Mediating conflict between interested crime victims and their offenders should receive far more attention from the large network of victim advocacy groups throughout the U.S. There is strong evidence that a victim's sense of vulnerability and anxiety can be reduced following a direct mediation session with their offender.

Program Implications

- A special unit on the victimization experience should be included in all training of mediators, preferably in cooperation with a local victim advocacy organization.
- Training of mediators should be enhanced to ensure that an appropriate non-directive style is used. This style includes the ability to make use of silence during mediation sessions, and to avoid missing opportunities to encourage either victim or offender to address emotional or informational issues that are important to them. Emphasis should be placed on demonstrated skill competency rather than simply completing a set number of hours of mediation training.
- New written and video training resources should be developed to highlight the importance of a non-directive style of mediation. These resources should provide specific examples of how to avoid missed opportunities for greater emotional closure for the victim and offender.
- Additional attention should be given to ensure that participation in mediation is voluntary for both parties. This should include training of case developers and mediators to inform parties of all available options prior to their choice of mediation.
- Programs should routinely require victims and offenders to sign a consent form, prior to the actual mediation session, that clearly explains mediation, states the voluntary nature of mediation and identifies other options that are available to the parties.
- The appropriate role of parents in the mediation process involving juvenile offenders needs additional clarification. Rather than ei-

ther a policy of including or not including parents in the actual session, programs should develop policies that identify for whom and under what specific circumstances parents should be allowed in the entire mediation session.

○ New written and video training resources should be developed to provide program staff and mediators assistance in identifying which cases and under what circumstances parental involvement in mediation is desirable. The manner in which parents are allowed to be in the mediation session, including additional ground rules, should be incorporated into these resources.

○ Case referral criteria in mediation programs should include both offenders with prior convictions and cases involving more serious offenses, such as residential burglary, robbery, aggravated assault and negligent homicide.

○ Programs should develop an ongoing system for collecting client satisfaction and other related data that is helpful for maintaining high quality control. This should include collecting data related to the participants' perception of voluntary participation, and to the role and effectiveness of the mediator. A program evaluation kit made available through this study could be helpful with such an effort.

LINGERING CRITICAL ISSUES

A number of critical issues face the field of victim-offender mediation as it continues to develop in North America and Europe. The four issues identified below are particularly important, even though other potential dangers certainly exist as well.

Losing the Vision

The possible loss of the underlying vision of restorative justice is perhaps the greatest danger facing this relatively young justice reform movement. Similar to other reform efforts, victim-offender mediation programs inevitably become preoccupied with securing more stable funding sources and developing more routine day-to-day operating procedures. It becomes increasingly easy to lose sight of the underlying values and principles that motivated the individuals who initiated the program, and that serve as the foundation for the program's existence. The importance of providing opportunities for addressing the emotional issues surrounding crime and victimization, including even the possibility of forgiveness and reconciliation, is a foundational principle of the field. To suggest that forgiveness and reconciliation may emerge spontaneously in some mediations is not to suggest that these principles be pushed upon the parties during their journey through the mediation process. Rather, if forgiveness and reconciliation occur, they must be genuinely owned and expressed by the victim and offender, without manipulation by the mediator. Losing sight of the restorative justice vision could easily result in a utilitarian and exclusive focus on simply determining restitution and payment, allowing little time for the sharing of information and feelings related to the crime, which can lead to a greater sense of closure for both parties.

Eliminating Pre-Mediation Sessions

Experience with thousands of cases over the past decade has consistently indicated that one of the most important impacts of the victim-offender mediation process is that of humanizing the justice system for both victim and offender. Victims are able to receive help in dealing with their emotional, informational, and material needs, while playing an active role in the process. Offenders learn of the real human impact of their actions, and are given an opportunity to make things right with their victims.

The process of contacting the victim and offender separately before the mediation session, through phone calls and usually a meeting, has proven to be essential to connecting with both parties, building trust and rapport, and encouraging their involvement in the most non-intimidating and understandable way possible.

In the haste to become more "efficient" and process more cases, it could become tempting to eliminate the important work that is required during the preparation for mediation phase. A number of programs have already moved in this direction; after all, "why bother with talking and meeting with them before mediation...the case will require a rather simple settlement...it's much more efficient to schedule a night when they can come to our office for the mediation." There certainly are some cases involving very minor offenses that may well not require separate meetings before the mediation. On the other hand, by eliminating the separate meetings and contacts with the parties on a more routine basis, the program is beginning to take on the charactersistics of the normal court system, which has little time to listen to victims and offenders or to respond to their needs. A focus on restitution agreements alone ignores the importance of the emotional and informational needs left in the wake of crime, which are central to a restorative justice perspective.

Taking the Easy Cases

As programs continue to be preoccupied with becoming acceptable, or institutionalized, the remaining two dangers grow out of a loss of vision. There can be a tremendous tendency to take few risks, particularly related to the type of cases being referred to the program. In one's eagerness to negotiate new referral arrangements and get enough cases, programs may be too quick to accept "garbage cases"—those that prosecutor's offices, in particular, either don't have sufficient evidence for or would prefer not being bothered with.

If victim-offender mediation becomes identified with primarily easy cases—those that the system would have done little with in the first place—the field will become increasingly marginalized and will not be taken seriously. It will remain on the margins, the sidelines, of how justice is done within communities.

Wider and Stronger Nets of Social Control

Restorative justice and of the victim-offender mediation field are deeply rooted in the idea of the mediation process as an alternative to the criminal justice system whenever possible. The VORP model of victim-offender mediation, as the most well-developed and documented model, was initially linked to the alternatives-to-incarceration movement during the late 1970s and early 1980s (Zehr and Umbreit, 1982), although this has not been emphasized as much during recent years. Taking the easy cases, many of which would not have even entered the formal criminal justice system, may push the field into the ranks of many other so-called alternatives that research has demonstrated have led to wider and stronger nets of social control (Austin and Krisberg, 1981; Dittenhoffer and Ericson, 1983). Despite intentions to the contrary, programs will be increasing—rather than limiting—state intervention into the lives of individuals who violate the law, many of whom the system would not have responded to because of the very minor nature of the offense. Rather than being an alternative to the system, these programs could result in additional sanctions for more offenders, with increasing overall cost to the justice system. While it is important to avoid unnecessary and costly "net widening" for relatively minor offenses, it is also important to realize that for many more serious offenses the mediation process is valid simply because it increases the quality of justice for the victim and the offender, even if a term of incarceration is a part of the sentence for more serious, particularly violent, offenses.

PRESENT OPPORTUNITIES

Dangers and pitfalls are faced by all social reform movements. Yet, by definition, the process of advocating and developing a reform program contains many creative opportunities.

Telling the Story

More than two decades of experience in bringing crime victims and their offenders face-to-face, and addressing a number of issues important to both parties, allows the field of victim-offender mediation to be in a stronger position than ever to boldly tell its story. There is no longer any question about whether victims would ever be willing to meet their offender. Nor is there any question about the intrinsic value of the mediation process in humanizing the criminal justice process, and promoting a greater sense of healing and closure for both victim and offender. Thousands of crime victims and offenders have benefited from the mediation process. Their individual stories offer powerful testimony to the basic validity of the model. These stories need to be increasingly heard by both the general public and policymakers. The stories of these individuals breathe life into the theory of restorative justice.

Working with Severely Violent Cases

Many programs have worked with simple assault cases from their inception, even while focusing their main effort on nonviolent property crime. The small but growing trend to have the victim-offender mediation process applied in more serious, violent cases represents a major opportunity to expand the impact and credibility of restorative justice (Gustafson and Smidstra, 1989; Umbreit, 1989b). This trend has been brought about by requests from people who have been victimized by such crimes as aggravated assault, armed robbery, sexual assault and attempted homicide. Mediation has also been requested by family members of homicide victims. Mediation in cases of severely violent criminal behavior has a number of distinguishing characteristics. These include:

- emotional intensity
- extreme need for non-judgmental attitude
- longer case preparation by mediator (8 to 12 months)
- multiple separate meetings prior to joint session
- multiple phone conversations
- negotiation with correctional officials to secure access to inmate and to conduct mediation in prison
- coaching of participants in the communication of intense feelings
- boundary clarification (mediation versus therapy)

The field is only beginning to come to grips with how the basic mediation model must be adapted to serve the more intense needs of parties involved in serious and violent criminal conflict. Far more extensive training of mediators is required, as is an entire new generation of written and audiovisual training resources. For example, mediators will need special knowledge and skills related to working with severely violent crimes, in addition to the normal mediation skills. From the victim's perspective, it will be important for the mediator to:

- understand the victimization experience/phases
- deal with grief and loss (our own and others)
- understand post-traumatic stress and its impact
- collaborate with psychotherapists

From the offender's perspective, mediators will need to:

- understand the criminal justice and corrections systems
- understand the offender's and prisoner's experiences
- relate to offenders convicted of heinous crimes in a non-judgmental manner
- negotiate with high-level correctional officials to gain access to the offender

A growing number of representatives of major victim advocacy organizations in different parts of the country are beginning to recognize the value of mediation for those victims of violence who express a need for it. As they directly confront the very source of terror in their lives, through mediation, some victims of violence are able to obtain a greater sense of healing and closure. The field of victim-offender mediation is faced with an exciting opportunity to stretch its original vision and significantly alter its original model to appropriately address the needs of parties affected by violent criminal conflict. This can only happen with: a serious commitment to re-examine the basic model and understanding its limitations; an increased awareness of the victimization experience, including posttraumatic stress and grieving; and a willingness to apply tighter boundaries to when mediation is appropriate, what kind of training is required, and who should serve as mediator(s). Far more extensive networking and coalition building with victim advocacy groups is also required.

Beyond Marginalization: The Primary Agenda as the Twenty-First Century Approaches

Marginalization is a major concern facing the entire field of victim-offender mediation in North America and Europe. Despite its growth and increasing acceptance, the practice of mediating conflict between crime victims and their offenders as part of the larger vision of restorative justice remains on the margins of how justice is pursued in modern industrialized western democracies. The basic principles of restorative justice require a fundamental shift in the power related to who controls and owns crime in society—a shift from the state to the individual citizen and local communities. While much of restorative justice has a good deal of popular appeal, the principles of retributive justice, focusing on state interests and the offender, still continue to drive criminal justice systems.

Moving the principles of restorative justice theory and the practice of victim-offender mediation from the margins to the mainstream of how we do justice in our society represents a major opportunity and challenge. Several important issues, however, will need to be addressed: wider public access to the mediation process; advocacy of mediation as a basic right for all victims; working with the media; and specific strategies for increasing case referrals to mediation.

Wider public access to the victim offender-mediation process must occur through public policy initiatives. With the growth of public—including victim—support, and the increase in empirical evidence supporting the multiple benefits of mediation, it is now time to give serious consideration to advocating mediation as a basic right of any crime victim in any community. This could be conditioned upon the availability of a competent mediator, the willingness of the parties and the absence of any major mental health issues.

Linkage of a strategy designed to broaden public access to mediation to only one side of the conflict (i.e., through victim rights' legislation), in an ideal setting, would not be preferable. Mediation, by definition, is meant to serve both parties in a fair and impartial manner. Promoting wider access to victim-offender mediation through linkage with victim rights' legislation would seem to be biased toward victims' concerns alone. Given the reality of criminal justice policy and public attitudes in most North American and European communities, however, no other strategy is more likely to greatly expand access to the mediation process for both crime victims and offenders. A recently passed victim bill of rights in Indiana became the first act of public policy to include these provisions (Stein, 1991).

Working effectively with the mass media is also an important issue. From the moment of birth, most of us are socialized in the belief that criminal conflict is, in the words of Christie (1981), the property of the state. We are, from a very early age through adulthood, bombarded with media images of cops and robbers. Many children's cartoons have themes of crime, violence and good conquering evil. Each year the prime-time television schedule includes police shows with intense action, adventure and violence. More recently, there has developed a series of television programs based on realistic recreations of actual crime incidents. These shows further project an adversarial perspective on crime and victimization, and reinforce commonly held stereotypes and images of criminals.

Restorative justice is based on very different principles than those that drive our current criminal justice systems. In fact, the values in which restorative justice is grounded run counter to dominant legal culture, which rests upon the foundation of an adversarial process and the need for professional dispute resolvers (i.e., lawyers). For the victim-offender mediation process, as the most visible expression of restorative justice, to move beyond marginalization it must become better known and embraced by popular culture. The mass media, and television particularly, are critical to the development of such a strategy. This should not, however, include allowing the media to exploit victims and offenders through the conducting of live mediations on television entertainment shows in front of an audience. To do so violates the integrity of the mediation process and could be harmful to the involved parties. However, collaborating with credible television documentaries or news magazine shows that respect the needs of mediation participants, including the private filming of mediation sessions if the parties approve, can be an effective educational tool.

The media represent a powerful force within society, whose influence upon public opinion and even value development can be enormous. In working with the media, however, it is extremely important to be careful, deliberate and assertive. Mediation programs must negotiate with the media so that their underlying interests and needs are met as much as possible. For example, programs must coach journalists in a clear and credible manner so that the message of the program comes across effectively to the general public. Mediation programs must always assume an active rather than passive role in working with the media.

While the issues of expanding access to victim-offender mediation through victim rights' legislation and working with the media are important long-term strategies that can move the field beyond its current marginalization, strategies that yield immediate short-term impact also need to be considered. The most obvious need is to address the fact that many victim-offender mediation programs receive only a small number of case referrals. Even those programs that receive 300 to 500 case referrals or more per year often have only a marginal impact on their local criminal justice system, when compared to the total number of cases in that jurisdiction.

For the victim-offender mediation process to be taken seriously and not continually marginalized, it must be able to demonstrate that it can work with a substantial volume of cases in a cost-effective manner through the use of trained community volunteers. Far more cases need to be referred to mediation as a true diversion from prosecution. In addition, more post-adjudication cases need to be referred either as a condition of probation or as a sole sanction alternative to traditional probation supervision. In fact, a presumptive referral to mediation strategy needs to be developed in most jurisdictions. Such a referral procedure would presume that all property offenses involving a restitution requirement would first be given the opportunity to participate in victim-offender mediation, rather than selecting out only certain cases for referral.

A number of specific strategies can be employed to increase case referrals to mediation programs (Umbreit, 1993c). The involvement and support of key criminal justice officials in the development and operation of the mediation program is critical to having cases referred to the program. Without the support of these officials, it is unlikely that the program will even be taken seriously, let alone receive an adequate number of referrals on a regular basis. Several strategies are offered for increasing the support of criminal justice officials for the program.

Strategy #1: Stakeholder Analysis

It will be important to conduct an analysis of the key stakeholders related to the development and operation of a victim-offender mediation program within the specific jurisdiction. Such an analysis should identify people by name and position, as well as indicate their level of support for mediation, who they are influenced by, and how any resistance can be overcome or at least neutralized. Key stakeholders usually include prosecutors, defense attorneys, judges, probation staff, victim advocates, offender advocates and court administrative staff. The importance of at least neutralizing opposition cannot be overemphasized. By simply meeting with the individuals, listening to their reasons for not supporting mediation enthusiastically, asking for any suggestions, and essentially agreeing to disagree on some points, it is possible to eliminate their active, vocal, and public opposition. (Appendix 5 features a stakeholder analysis form.)

Strategy #2: Advisory Committee

In order to increase justice system involvement in the program, an advisory committee of key justice system representatives should be organized. This committee might meet two to four times a year. It could both increase support for the program, and provide helpful feedback and guidance.

Strategy #3: Presentations/Mini-Seminar

Presentations should be scheduled at regular meetings of prosecuting attorneys, defense attorneys, judges, probation staff and other referral sources. Going to their "turf" is most likely to gain the attendance and attention of these key players. It might also be wise to schedule presentations and provide updates about the program on an annual basis for the key referral source. In addition, a good strategy during the early development of the program is that of a luncheon mini-seminar on victim-offender mediation, to which key people from the community, the political system and the criminal justice system are invited. While the presentations at meetings of key referral sources are likely to be brief (15 to 30 minutes), the luncheon mini-seminar could be two hours long. A guest speaker or consultant who is familiar with the field could present a larger perspective on how the field of victim-offender mediation is developing and the impact it is having. Or, a presentation by local staff or board could be made in conjunction with a videotape of a mediation or testimony by several victims or offenders who have gone through mediation and felt good about it. It would also be beneficial to have the media present at this type of event.

While the above strategies for increasing system support for the program will provide both short- and long-term benefits, they are unlikely to result in an immediate increase in the number of cases being referred to the program. Verbal endorsement of the program by key referral sources should never be confused with actually receiving case referrals. To receive more cases, an assertive and cooperative communication strategy must be employed to help a large bureaucracy change the manner in which it understands and responds to crime. This is no easy task. One should never assume that good intentions and philosophical support for mediation is equated with more referrals. Similarly, one should not assume that the lack of referrals means that the referral source doesn't really support the concept of mediation and restorative justice, despite verbal statements to the contrary. More often than not, the lack of referrals received by victim-offender mediation programs has more to do with the program itself and the communication strategies it uses than it does with the larger system actively resisting the concept. If the program staff make it easy for the referral source to send cases, and the referral source sees it in their interest to reduce their caseload, most referral sources will eventually send plenty of cases, sometimes even too many.

Several strategies for developing a more assertive and proactive process of case referral are offered.

Strategy #4: Victim Encouragement Letter or Flyer

A brief victim-oriented letter, flyer or card should be developed and given to referral sources for them to routinely provide to victims that are being contacted about the mediation program. The more direct or indirect contact that the program has in presenting the mediation concept to victims, the more likely that victims will participate. When persons who are unfamiliar with the victim-offender mediation concept—or even resistant to it—have initial contact with the victim, it is quite likely that they will not do a good job of encouraging victims to consider the benefits of mediation. This victim encouragement letter could be mailed to victims with the letter that is usually sent to inform them that their case has been referred to the program, and that a representative from the program will be contacting them. Or, the encouragement letter could be handed out to the victim during the initial individual meeting with the victim that occurs in the vast majority of victim-offender mediation programs. If during the initial phone call with the victim he or she seems skeptical about mediation and is probably not likely to even agree to an individual meeting with the mediator, the victim encouragement letter could also be mailed to them (if it has not already been sent) prior to calling them back at a later point. By giving the victim more time to think about mediation, along with a brief and persuasive letter/flyer, the likelihood of the victim agreeing during the next phone conversation to a separate meeting with the mediator, if not mediation itself, increases. (Appendix 6 features an example of a victim encouragement letter.)

Strategy #5: Weekly Phone Calls and Office Visits

In order to maintain a constant presence with key referral sources and to keep them continually aware of the program and its openness to referrals, weekly phone calls should be made to key contacts. Each key contact need not be called each week, but calls should be made each week to several key people who could make direct referrals. These calls are most likely going to be made to probation staff and prosecuting attorneys who work with a large caseload. The calls should be brief and made in a pleasant tone in which contacts are asked if they have any current cases that might be appropriate for referral to mediation. In addition to periodic phone calls to key referral contacts, periodic visits to the offices of the referral source are important. These can be brief; their purpose is simply to have the program and its representative become more known to staff at the agency.

CONCLUDING REMARKS

In addition to the aforementioned opportunities facing the field of victim-offender mediation, several others also exist. With its many years of experience, the field can now take the lead in: developing standards of practice; certifying mediators; greater networking among colleagues in North America and Europe; initiating longitudinal studies to assess the long-term impact of mediation; and conducting cross-national studies to gain a greater understanding of the development of the victim-offender mediation process in differing national and cultural contexts.

Restorative justice theory and the practice of victim-offender mediation represent extremely important contributions to how we understand and respond to crime in modern industrialized democracies. By viewing certain types of criminal behavior as conflicts between individuals within community settings, rather than exclusively focusing upon state interests, the victim-offender mediation movement in North America and Europe represents a challenging new vision of how communities can respond to crime and victimization. Such a strong emphasis upon restoration and healing rather than retribution and revenge may seem too radical for some. However, the vision of restorative justice, particularly as applied through the practice of victim-offender mediation, is far from being a radical new concept. Rather, such a vision of doing justice in contemporary society is deeply rooted in many of the religious and secular traditions that are part of our collective heritage. Throughout the centuries, these traditions have emphasized the importance of viewing criminal behavior as conflict between individuals, while stressing the value of direct accountability, remorse, forgiveness and reconciliation, whenever possible.

AUTHOR'S NOTE: The section on strategies to increase case referrals to programs in order to move beyond marginalization represents excerpts from a publication by the author for *The Network: Interaction for Conflict Resolution*, Ontario, CAN. Permission has been received from The Network for use of this material.

References

Austin, J. and B. Krisberg (1981). "Wider, Stronger, and Different Nets: The Dialectics of Criminal Justice Reform." *Journal of Research in Crime and Delinquency* 18(1):165-196.

Bae, I. (1991). "A Survey on Public Acceptance of Restitution as an Alternative to Incarceration for Property Offenders in Hennepin County, Minnesota." In: Heinz Messmer and Hans-Uwe Otto (eds.), *Restorative Justice on Trial*. Dordrecht, NETH: Kluwer Academic Publishers.

Bazemore, S.G. (1990). *Accountability in Juvenile Justice: What It Is, What It Isn't*. Walnut Creek, CA: Pacific Institute for Research & Evaluation.

—— (1992). "On Mission Statements and Reform in Juvenile Justice: The Case of the 'Balanced Approach.'" *Federal Probation* 56(3):64-70.

Braithwaite, J. (1989). *Crime, Shame and Reintegration*. Cambridge, MA: Cambridge University Press.

Butts, J.A. and H.N. Snyder (1991). *Restitution and Juvenile Recidivism*. Pittsburgh, PA: National Center for Juvenile Justice.

Christie, N. (1981). *Limits to Pain*. Oslo, NOR: Universitetsforlaget. Distributed in the U.S. by Columbia University Press.

Clarke, P. (1985). *Perception of Criminal Justice Surveys: Executive Summary*. The Michigan Prison and Jail Overcrowding Project.

Coates, R.B. and J. Gehm (1985). *Victim Meets Offender: An Evaluation of Victim Offender Reconciliation Programs*. Valparaiso, IN: PACT Institute of Justice.

—— and J. Gehm (1989). "An Empirical Assessment." In: M. Wright and B. Galaway (eds.), *Mediation and Criminal Justice*. London: Sage Publications.

Collins, J.P. (1983). *Final Evaluation Report of the Lethbridge Alternative Disposition Project for Young Offenders*. Ottawa, CAN: Consultation Centre (Prairies), Ministry of the Solicitor General of Canada.

—— (1984). *Evaluation Report: Grande Prairie Reconciliation Project for Young Offenders*. Ottawa, CAN: Consultation Centre (Prairies), Ministry of the Solicitor General of Canada.

Davis, G., J. Boucherat and D. Watson (1988). "Reparation in the Service of Diversion: the Subordination of a Good Idea." *Howard Journal of Criminal Justice* 27 (2):127-134.

Davis, R., M. Tichane and D. Grayson (1980). *Mediation and Arbitration as Alternative to Prosecution in Felony Arrest Cases: An Evaluation of the Brooklyn Dispute Resolution Center.* New York: VERA Institute of Justice.

Denzin, N.K. (1978). *The Research Act.* New York: McGraw-Hill.

Dignan, J. (1990). *Repairing the Damage.* Sheffield, UK: Centre for Criminological and Legal Research, University of Sheffield.

Dittenhoffer, T. and R. Ericson (1983). "The Victim Offender Reconciliation Program: A Message to Correctional Reformers." *University of Toronto Law Journal* 33(3):315-347.

Fagan H., and Gehm, J. (1993). *Victim-Offender Reconciliation and Mediation Program Directory.* Valparaiso, IN: PACT Institute of Justice.

Fischer, D.G. and R. Jeune (1987). "Juvenile Diversion: A Process Analysis." *Canadian Psychology* 28:60-70.

Galaway, B. (1988). "Crime Victim and Offender Mediation as a Social Work Strategy." *Social Service Review* 62:668-683.

—— (1989). "Informal Justice: Mediation Between Offenders and Victims." In: P.A. Albrecht and O. Backes (eds.), *Crime Prevention and Intervention: Legal and Ethical Problems.* Berlin: Walter de Gruyter.

—— and J. Hudson. *Criminal Justice, Restitution, and Reconciliation.* Monsey, NY: Criminal Justice Press.

Gehm, J. (1990). "Mediated Victim-Offender Restitution Agreements: An Exploratory Analysis of Factors Related to Victim Participation." In: B. Galaway and J. Hudson (eds.), *Criminal Justice, Restitution and Reconciliation.* Monsey, NY: Criminal Justice Press.

Gottfredson, S.D., B.D. Warner and R.B. Taylor (1988). "Conflict and Consensus about Criminal Justice in Maryland." In: N. Walker and M. Hough (eds.), *Public Attitudes to Sentencing: Surveys from Five Countries.* Aldershot, UK: Gower.

Glazer, B.G. and A. Strauss (1967). *The Discovery of Grounded Theory.* Chicago: Aldine.

Guedalia, L.J. (1979). Predicting Recidivism of Juvenile Delinquents on Restitutionary Probation from Selected Background, Subject and Program Variables. Unpublished dissertation. American University, Washington, DC.

Gustafson, D.L. and H. Smidstra (1989). *Victim Offender Reconciliation in Serious Crime: A Report on the Feasibility Study Undertaken for The*

Ministry of the Solicitor General (Canada). Langley, BC: Fraser Region Community Justice Insititatives Association.

Hughes, S.P. and A.L. Schneider (1989). "Victim-Offender Mediation: A Survey of Program Characteristics and Perceptions of Effectiveness." *Crime & Delinquency* 35(2):217-233.

Mackey, V. (1990). *Restorative Justice, Toward Nonviolence.* Louisville, KY: Presbyterian Criminal Justice Program.

Mauer, M. (1991). *Americans Behind Bars: A Comparison of International Rates of Incarceration.* Washington, DC: The Sentencing Project.

Marshall, T.F. and S. Merry (1990). *Crime and Accountability.* London: Home Office.

Messmer, H. and Hans-Uwe Otto (1992). *Restorative Justice on Trial: Pitfalls and Potentials of Victim-Offender Mediation—International Research Perspectives.* Dordrecht, NETH: Kluwer.

Miles, M.B. and A.M. Huberman (1984). *Qualitative Data Analysis.* Beverly Hills, CA: Sage Publications.

Patton, M.Q. (1980). *Qualitative Evaluation Methods.* Beverly Hills, CA: Sage Publications.

Perry, L., T. Lajeunesse and A. Woods (1987). *Mediation Services: An Evaluation.* Manitoba, CAN: Research, Planning and Evaluation, Office of the Attorney General.

Pranis, K. and M.S. Umbreit (1992). *Public Opinion Research Challenges Perception of Widespread Public Demand for Harsher Punishment.* Minneapolis, MN: Citizens Council.

Public Agenda Foundation (1987). *Crime and Punishment: The Public's View.* New York: Edna McConnell Clark Foundation.

—— (1989). *Punishing Criminals: The Public's View, An Alabama Survey.* New York: Edna McConnell Clark Foundation.

—— (1991). *Punishing Criminals: The People of Delaware Consider the Options.* New York: Edna McConnell Clark Foundation.

Public Opinion Research (1986). *Report Prepared for the North Carolina Center on Crime and Punishment.* Washington, DC.

Schneider, A.L. and P.R. Schneider (1984). "Comparison of Programmatic and 'Ad Hoc' Restitution." *Justice Quarterly* 1:529-547.

—— ed. (1985). *Guide to Juvenile Restitution.* Washington, DC: Office of Juvenile Justice and Delinquency Prevention.

—— (1986). "Restitution and Recidivism Rates of Juvenile Offenders: Results from Four Experimental Studies." *Criminology* 24(3):533-552.

—— and D.D. Schram (1986). "The Washington State Juvenile Justice Reform: A Review of Findings." *Criminal Justice Policy Review* 1(2):211-235.

Stein, Mark (1991). "Mediation as a Victim Right." *Victim Offender Mediation*, A newsletter of the U.S. Association for Victim Offender Mediation. Valparaiso, IN: PACT Institute of Justice.

Umbreit, M.S. (1985). *Crime and Reconciliation: Creative Options for Victims and Offenders*. Nashville, TN: Abingdon Press.

—— (1986a). "Victim Offender Mediation: A National Survey. *Federal Probation* 50(4):53-56.

—— (1986b). "Victim Offender Mediation and Judicial Leadership." *Judicature* 69(4):202-204.

—— (1988). "Mediation of Victim Offender Conflict." *Journal of Dispute Resolution* 85-105.

—— (1989a). "Victims Seeking Fairness, Not Revenge: Toward Restorative Justice." *Federal Probation* 53(3):52-57.

—— (1989b). "Violent Offenders and Their Victims." In: M. Wright and B. Galaway (eds.), *Mediation and Criminal Justice*. London: Sage Publications.

—— (1990). "The Meaning of Fairness to Burglary Victims." In: B. Galaway and J. Hudson (eds.), *Criminal Justice, Restitution and Reconciliation*. Monsey, NY: Criminal Justice Press.

—— (1991a). "Mediating Victim Offender Conflict: From Single-Site to Multi-Site Analysis in the U.S." In: H. Messmer and H.-U. Otto (eds.), *Restorative Justice on Trial*. Dordrecht, NETH: Kluwer Academic Publishers.

—— (1991b). "Having Offenders Meet With Their Victim Offers Benefits for both Parties." *Corrections Today* (July):164-166.

—— (1991c). "Minnesota Mediation Center Gets Positive Results." *Corrections Today* (August):194-197.

—— and R.B. Coates (1992). "The Impact of Mediating Victim Offender Conflict: An Analysis of Programs in Three States." *Juvenile & Family Court Journal* 43:21-28.

—— (1993a). "Crime Victims and Offenders in Mediation: An Emerging Area of Social Work Practice." *Social Work* 38(1):69-73.

—— (1993b). "Juvenile Offenders Meet Their Victims: The Impact of Mediation in Albuquerque, New Mexico." *Family and Conciliation Courts Review* 31(1):90-100.

—— and R.B. Coates (1993c). "Cross-Site Analysis of Victim Offender Mediation in Four States." *Crime & Delinquency* 39(4):565-585.

Van Ness, D.W. (1986). *Crime and Its Victims*. Downers Grove, IL: Intervarsity Press.

—— D. Carlson, T. Crawford and K. Strong (1989). *Restorative Justice Theory*. Washington, DC: Justice Fellowship.

Wright, M. and B. Galaway (1989). *Mediation and Criminal Justice*. London: Sage.

—— (1991). *Justice for Victims and Offenders*. Philadelphia, PA: Open University Press.

Zehr, H. (1980). *Mediation the Victim-Offender Conflict*. Akron, PA: Mennonite Central Committee.

—— (1990). *Changing Lenses, A New Focus for Crime and Justice*. Scottsdale, PA: Herald Press.

—— and M. Umbreit (1982). "Victim Offender Reconciliation: An Incarceration Substitute?" *Federal Probation* 46:63-68.

List of Written/Audiovisual Resources: Victim-Offender Mediation

TRAINING AND TECHNICAL ASSISTANCE MANUALS

The VORP Book: An Organizational and Operations Manual
This is the most comprehensive technical assistance manual on initiating and managing victim-offender mediation and reconciliation programs. It includes chapters on: an overview of the process; an organizer's handbook; volunteer training; case and information management; and moving toward an urban/multicultural setting. Available for $25 through the PACT Institute of Justice, 254 S. Morgan Blvd., Valparaiso, IN 46383; (219) 462-1127.

Victim-Offender Mediation Training Package
This comprehensive victim-offender mediation package includes one trainer's manual, two coach's manuals, ten training and resource manuals, and one training video (60 min.). The entire package costs $470.00 (CAN). The cost of the components if purchased separately include: trainer's manual, $95; coach's manual, $15; training and resource manual, $25; and the training video, $95. Available from Community Justice Initiatives Association, 101 — 20678 Eastleigh Crescent, Langley, BC V3A 4C4 CAN; (604) 534-5515.

TRAINING VIDEOS

Available from:
• Center for Creative Justice, 304 Lynn Ave., Ames, IA 50010; (515) 292-3820

º Community Justice Initiatives Association (Langley)

º PACT Institute of Justice (Valparaiso)

DIRECTORY

Victim-Offender Reconciliation & Mediation Directory. Harriet Fagan and Johm Gehm (1993). PACT Institute of Justice, 254 S. Morgan Blvd., Valparaiso, IN 46383.

BOOKS

Changing Lenses. Howard Zehr (1990). Herald Press, Scottdale, PA 15683.

Crime and Accountability, Victim Offender Mediation in Practice. Tony Marshall and Susan Merry (1990). Home Office, P.O. Box 276, London, SW8 5DT, UK.

Crime and Reconciliation: Creative Options for Victims and Offenders. Mark S. Umbreit (1985). Abingdon Press, P.O. Box 801, Nashville, TN 37202.

Crime and Its Victims. Dan W. Van Ness (1986). Intervarsity Press, Downers Grove, IL.

Criminal Justice, Restitution, and Reconciliation. Burt Galaway and Joe Hudson (1990). Criminal Justice Press, 124 Willow Tree Road, P.O. Box 249, Monsey, NY 10952.

Justice for Victims and Offenders. Martin Wright (1991). Open University Press, Philadelphia, PA.

Mediation and Criminal Justice. Martin Wright and Burt Galaway (1989). Sage Publications, 2111 West Hillcrest Drive, Newbury Park, CA 91320.

Victim Meets Offender: The Impact of Restorative Justice and Mediation. Mark S. Umbreit (available in 1994). Criminal Justice Press, 124 Willow Tree Road, P.O. Box 249, Monsey, NY 10952.

PAMPHLETS

How To Increase Referrals to Victim Offender Mediation Programs. Mark Umbreit (1993). Fund for Dispute Resolution, c/o Conrad Grebal College, Waterloo, Ontario, CAN N2L 3G6.

Justice: The Restorative Vision. Howard Zehr, Dan Van Ness and M. Kay Harris (1989). Mennonite Central Committee, Akron, PA 17501.

Mediating the Victim Offender Conflict. Howard Zehr (1982). Mennonite Central Committee, Akron, PA 17501.

Retributive Justice, Restorative Justice. Howard Zehr (1985). Mennonite Central Committee, Akron, PA 17501.

VORP Organizing: A Foundation in the Church. Ron Claassen and Howard Zehr with Duane Ruth-Heffelbower (1989). Mennonite Central Committee U.S., Office of Criminal Justice, 107 W. Lexington Ave., Elkhart, IN 46516.

JOURNAL ARTICLES

"Crime Victim and Offender Mediation As A Social Work Strategy," Burt Galaway. *Social Service Review*, Vol. 62, 1988.

"Crime Victims and Offenders in Mediation: An Emerging Area of Social Work Practice," Mark S. Umbreit. *Social Work*, Vol. 38, No.1, 1993.

"Cross-Site Analysis of Victim Offender Mediation in Four States," Mark S. Umbreit and Robert B. Coates. *Crime & Delinquency*, October 1993.

"Having Offenders Meet With Their Victims Offers Benefits for Both Parties," *Corrections Today* July, 1991.

"The Impact of Mediating Victim Offender Conflict: An Analysis of Programs in Three States," Mark S. Umbreit and Robert B. Coates. *Juvenile & Family Court Journal*, Vol. 43, No.1, 1992.

"Juvenile Diversion: A Process Analysis," D.G. Fischer and R. Jeune (1987). *Canadian Psychology*, Vol. 28.

"Juvenile Offenders Meet Their Victims: The Impact of Mediation in Albuquerque, New Mexico," Mark S. Umbreit. *Family and Conciliation Courts Review*, Vol. 31, No.1, 1993.

"Mediation of Victim Offender Conflict," Mark S. Umbreit. *Journal of Dispute Resolution*, 1988.

"Minnesota Mediation Center Produces Positive Results," Mark S. Umbreit. *Corrections Today*, August, 1991.

"Restitution as Innovation or Unfilled Promise?" Burt Galaway. *Federal Probation*, Vol. 52, No.3, 1988.

"Restitution and Recidivism Rates of Juvenile Offenders: Results from Four Experimental Studies," Anne L. Schneider. *Criminology*, Vol. 24, No.3, 1986.

"Restitution As Innovation or Unfilled Promise?" Burt Galaway. *Federal Probation*, Vol. 52, No.3, 1988.

"The Victim Offender Reconciliation Program: A Message to Correctional Reformers," Tony Dittenhoffer and Richard Ericson. *University of Toronto Law Journal*, Vol. 33, No.3, 1983.

"Victim Offender Mediation: A National Survey," Mark S. Umbreit. *Federal Probation*, December, 1986.

"Victim-Offender Mediation: A Survey of Program Characteristics and Perceptions of Effectiveness," Stella P. Hughes and Anne L. Schneider. *Crime & Delinquency*, Vol. 46, No.2, 1989.

"Victim Offender Reconciliation: An Incarceration Substitute?" Howard Zehr and Mark S. Umbreit. *Federal Probation*, Vol. 46, No.4, 1982.

"Victims Seeking Fairness, Not Revenge: Toward Restorative Justice," Mark S. Umbreit. *Federal Probation*, September, 1989.

RESOURCE ORGANIZATIONS

Victim Offender Mediation Association

(includes programs throughout North America)

c/o PACT Institute of Justice

254 S. Morgan Blvd. Valparaiso, IN 46383

(219) 462-1127

Victim Offender Ministries Program

Mennonite Central Committee Canada

50 Kent Avenue

Kitchener, Ontario N2G 3R1, CAN

(519) 745-8458

Office of Criminal Justice

Mennonite Central Committee U.S.

P.O. Box 500, Akron, PA 17501

(717) 859-3889

For additional information related to program development, technical assistance, mediation training or research, contact:

Mark S. Umbreit, Ph.D.

School of Social Work

University of Minnesota

383 McNeal Hall, 1985 Buford Ave.

St. Paul, MN 55108

(612) 624-3700

Appendix 1. Research Plan for Cross-Site Analysis of Victim-Offender Mediation

RESEARCH QUESTIONS	DATA COLLECTED	DATA SOURCES	DATA INSTRU- MENTS	ANALYSIS
1. Who participates in the victim-offender mediation process and why?	Client demographics Reasons for participation	Mediation clients Program records	Participant log sheets Coding schedule for record data Interview schedule	Quantitative Qualitative
2. How does the process work, and what is the role and function of the mediator?	Project plans and accomplish- ments Project activities	Program records Mediators	Coding schedule for record data Interview schedule Observation protocols	Qualitative
3. How do participants in the mediation process evaluate it?	Expression of client satisfaction or dissat- isfaction	Mediation clients	Likert scales Interview schedule	Quantitative Qualitative
4. What do court officials think about mediation?	Expression of satisfaction or dissatisfac- tion	Court officials	Interview schedule	Quantitative Qualitative

RESEARCH QUESTIONS	DATA COLLECTED	DATA SOURCES	DATA INSTRU- MENTS	ANALYSIS
5. What were the immediate outcomes of the victim- offender mediation process?	Number of mediation sessions Number of restitution agreements Amount/type of restitution	Mediation clients Program records Program staff	Interview schedule Coding schedule for record data Interview schedule	Quantitative Qualitative
6. What is the impact of mediation on restitution completion rates?	Amount of res- titution Impact on vic- tim/offender attitudes and perceptions Case closed- out information	Program records Court records	Coding schedule for record data	Quantitative
7. What is the impact of mediation on recidivism?	Criminal offenses committed within a one- year period	Court records	Coding schedule for record data	Quantitative
8. What are the cost implications?	Unit cost of processing referrals Unit cost of mediation	Program records	Coding schedule for record data	Quantitative
9. What is the meaning of *fairness* to victims and offenders in mediation?	Attitudes and perceptions of victims and offenders	Mediation clients	Interview schedule	Qualitative

Appendix 2. Cost Implications of Victim-Offender Mediation Programs

• *Average unit cost of a case referral was $233*
• *Average unit cost of a mediation case was $678*

The annual cost of operating the three primary programs examined in this study, during 1991, ranged from $31,530 in Albuquerque to $127,176 in Oakland. By far the largest single-cost item was that of personnel, representing a range of 69% of the budget in Albuquerque to 72% in Minnesota and Oakland. The average amount of staff at these programs was 2.8 FTEs.

The unit cost of a referral to these programs during 1991 ranged from $81 in Albuquerque to $346 in Oakland. For those cases that were referred to the program and that later participated in a mediation session, the unit cost of a mediation ranged from $292 in Minneapolis to $986 in Oakland.

All three programs operated as a unit within a larger private, non-profit agency, which provided many different types of support and financial assistance. This relationship appeared to be crucial during both the initial development of each program and the subsequent years, when there were periodic gaps in the flow of revenue to directly support the victim-offender mediation program. As Table 17 indicates, the cost implications of operating these three programs differed considerably.

Tables 18 through 20 provide a more detailed description of program costs at each site, for 1990 and 1991 separately. These tables are based on actual expenses and are particularly helpful in identifying the range of specific cost items, such as staff positions, rent, telephone, printing, etc., as well as of indirect expenses related to administrative overhead. The amount of indirect costs at the various program sites ranged from a low of 8.7% of direct program expenses in Minneapolis, to a high of 31% in Albuquerque. It is important to realize, however, that "indirect costs" are defined differently at the program sites. For example, in Minneapolis certain indirect type of expenses such as a portion of the salary of some support staff are listed as direct program expenses, whereas at the other two sites this is not the case.

Table 17: Cost of Victim-Offender Mediation Programs (Based on 1991 Expenses)

ITEM	ALBUQUER-QUE	MINNEA-POLIS	OAKLAND	TOTAL
Personnel cost	$21,753	$88,493	$91,884	$202,130
Number of staff	1.5 FTE	3.5 FTE	3.5 FTE	8.5 FTE
Other program costs	$9,777	$34,873	$35,322	$79,972
Total annual cost	$31,530	$123,366	$127,176	$282,072
Annual cases referred	391	453	368	1,212
Unit cost of referral	$81	$272	$346	$233
Annual cases mediated	108	179	129	416
Unit cost of mediation	$292	$689	$986	$678

Table 18: Minneapolis Program Costs

	1990	1991
Personnel Costs		
1. Program Director	.80 FTE	.65 FTE
2. Staff Mediators	1.63 FTE	2.30 FTE
3. Secretary	.40 FTE	.40 FTE
4. Other Support Staff	.21 FTE	.20 FTE
Total Full-Time Equivalent	3.04 FTE	3.55 FTE
Total Salary Costs	$68,190	$76,275
Total Fringe Benefits/Taxes	$10,667	$12,218
SUBTOTAL	$78,857	$88,493
Other Operating Costs		
Rent	$9,195	$9,326
Supplies	1,288	1,140
Telephone	1,530	2,158
Postage	475	394
Printing	1,103	545
Conferences	3,238	2,911
Miscellaneous	2,270	2,467
SUBTOTAL	$19,099	$18,941
Travel Costs	3,311	4,093
Other Direct Costs		
Depreciation	$ 1,987	$ 1,788
Total Direct Costs	$103,254	$113,315
Indirect Costs (8.7% and 8.9%)	8,962	10,051
TOTAL EXPENSES	$112,216	$123,366

Table 19: Oakland Program Costs

	1990	1991
Personnel Costs		
1. Program Director	.90 FTE	.90 FTE
2. Senior Case Coor-dinator	1.00 FTE	1.00 FTE
3. Training Coordin-ator		.60 FTE
4. Project Organizer (VISTA-type volunteer)	1.00 FTE	1.00 FTE
Total Full-Time Equivalent	2.90 FTE	3.50 FTE
Total Salary Costs	$58,028	$74,678
Total Fringe Bene-fits/Taxes	$13,346	$17,176
SUBTOTAL	$71,374	$91,854
Other Operating Costs		
Rent	$4,680	$4,933
Supplies	600	800
Telephone	250	250
Postage	700	900
Printing	1,000	1,350
SUBTOTAL	$7,230	$8,233
Travel Costs	$1,000	$1,500
Training of Mediators	$500	$3,000
Total Direct Costs	$80,104	$104,587
Indirect Costs (21%)	$17,222	$22,584
TOTAL EXPENSES	$97,326	$127,176

Table 20: Albuquerque Program Costs

	1990 7/1-12/31	1991 1/1-6/30
Personnel Costs		
1. Program Director	1.00 FTE	1.00 FTE
2. Program Assistant	.50 FTE	.50 FTE
Total Full-Time Equivalent	1.50 FTE	1.50 FTE
Total Salary Costs	$9,935	$10,676
Total Fringe Benefits/Taxes	$612	$530
SUBTOTAL	$10,547	$11,206
Other Operating Costs		
Rent	$91	$90
Supplies	176	175
Telephone	211	211
Postage	108	108
Printing	136	136
SUBTOTAL	$722	$720
Travel Costs	$161	$150
Volunteer Costs		
Training	$98	$120
Mileage Reimbursed	80	95
SUBTOTAL	$178	$215
Other Direct Costs		
Accounting	$94	$94
Total Direct Costs	$11,702	$12,385
Indirect Costs (31%)	3,721	3,721
TOTAL EXPENSES	$15,424	$16,106

Appendix 3. Parental Involvement in Victim-Offender Mediation

Children have parents. An obvious fact, but one that can create havoc or harmony in victim-offender mediation involving juveniles, because of the diversity of the child-parent relationship. The relationship between a child and his/her parent(s) may be beneficial or destructive—towards their child; towards the victim or offender in mediation; and towards the mediation process—all independent of each other. For example, a child may have a critical, overbearing parent who supports the mediation process, believing the child should do restitution for what she/he has done, but who does not support their child, and is indifferent to the needs of the victim. In any case, the involvement of parents in the mediation process makes a difficult process even more complex.

A child-parent relationship exists and influences the mediation process whether the parent is present or not. This influence occurs between the parent and child, as well as among the parent(s), and the mediator and the mediation process. In regard to the parental influence on the child, mediation pays special attention to the existence of any power imbalance among the parties in dispute. When parents are invited to be present during a mediation session, the power imbalance inherent in the parent-child relationship is likely to also be present. In addition, the concept of parental rights influences the mediator and the possibilities for mediation, as parents do have specific legal and social rights that they may invoke at any time before, during or after mediation. An example of this is a mediation case in which the father was dissatisfied with the signed agreement, and he requested and received additional mediation sessions to change the outcome of the mediation process.

In addition to the parental influences on a psychological level with the child, and a social and legal level for the mediator and mediation process, there is also the potential for additional conflicts arising between the parents of the victim and the parents of the offender. This additional conflict, separate from the original conflict that required mediation intervention, may be the result of trying to protect the child, or of unrelated and unresolved parental issues. With parental involvement, a two-child conflict in mediation can increase to include the victim's and offender's natural parents and stepparents, each with their own agenda and concept of justice.

There are other influences that parental involvement has on the mediation process, such as cultural and racial bias, ethnic diversity, and unresolved issues of the parent that are acted out through or by the child. The following information presents the themes that were extracted from the results of open-ended interviews conducted at three research sites—California, Minnesota, and New Mexico.

METHODOLOGY

The findings that emerged from the research sites are divided into quantitative data and qualitative data. The quantitative data is presented in Table 21, and the major findings are highlighted. The qualitative data presents important themes, along with illustrative quotes that further explain the theme. The themes presented in the qualitative data analysis are defined as positive or negative based upon the victims' viewpoints of parental involvement. The results are presented from the most frequent number of responses that stated a similar viewpoint, to the least frequent. The offenders' viewpoints are presented in one section because of the small sample size.

It is important to keep in mind that the findings of the research are preliminary and not exhaustive. Nor are all the possible issues of parental involvement and influence mentioned or discussed.

QUANTITATIVE DATA

To determine the extent of parental involvement in the mediation process, the victim was asked, "Who was present at the mediation session?" There were 137 responses to this question, which represented 137 mediations. Table 21 identifies how the 137 responses were distributed among the three sites.

Overall, parental participation occurred in over 50% of the mediation cases, with a wide variation in actual participation, from a low of 19% in New Mexico, to a high of 82% in California. The data do not explain why there is such a wide variation in parental participation. In addition, mothers attended mediation sessions more often than fathers, except in New Mexico which had an equal number, however, this result is not reliable because of the small sample size. Finally, there were more cases with one parent attending than with both parents. California had the highest parental participation in all categories, and New Mexico had the lowest participation level in all categories, although, once again, the data does not explain this variation.

Table 21: Parental Presence in Mediation Session

VARIABLE	MINNEA-POLIS	ALBUQUER-QUE	OAKLAND	TOTAL
Parent(s) in mediation	66	37	34	137
(1 or more present)	48% of total	27% of total	25% of total	100%
a. One parent only	42 (64%)	7 (19%)	28 (82%)	77(56%)
b. Both parents	14 (21%)	1 (3%)	12 (35%)	27(20%)
c. Mother present	35 (53%)	4 (10%)	22 (65%)	61 (45%)
d. Father present	22 (33%),	4 (10%)	17 (50%)	43 (31%)

QUALITATIVE DATA

The methodology used to gather and analyze the qualitative data involved a two step process. First, all interview responses of 25 open-ended questions for victims and 15 opened-ended questions for offenders were systematically recorded from the three research sites—California, Minnesota and New Mexico. Second, the recorded answers were examined for parental references, by using key words and phrases, such as parent, mother, father and dad. The results of examining the qualitative data are presented in the following sections.

THEMES OF PARENTAL INVOLVEMENT IN MEDIATION

A particular theme was identified in an interview write-up if it was explicitly mentioned at least once by a respondent, however, none of the questions directly asked about parental involvement. For example, a question was asked about what was least or most satisfying about the mediation process, and the respondents would comment about the parental involvement. The open-ended questions did not direct the victims or offenders to comment about the parental involvement, so all the information presented was volunteered. For example, least satisfying was, "Not being able to hear the son [offender] because of the father."

Victim's Positive Themes

Victims expressed several positive aspects of having the offender's parents involved in the mediation process. These positive responses included being satisfied with meeting the parents; having the parents help with restitution; and being able to explain their viewpoint of what happened to the parents.

Offender's parents positive influence on mediation (n=19):

In general, when victims directly addressed the importance of parental involvement, they did so in a positive way. These comments included expressing satisfaction that the parents were involved and open to the mediation process. Comments to this affect included, "The boy and his mom were very concerned in getting things straightened out." "Fairness means getting to meet the offender's parents and talking over what happened." "The kids are so little. It's up to the parents to punish the kids." "Maybe having the parents involved will prevent it from happening again."

Offender's parents responsible for restitution (n=11):

Some of the victims believed that the parents of the offenders were responsible for restitution. Such comments referred to the fairness, ease and timeliness of the restitution. Examples included, "I should have been paid back immediately by her parents." "I'll be thrilled if the parents come through with the agreed upon amount." "Just the uncooperative parent ... wouldn't pay her share." "That each of the offender's parents comes up with the restitution. Even if the parents have to take loans."

Offender's parents hear about offender's actions (n=8):

Some victims wanted to be heard and expressed concern that the parents should be aware of the offender's actions. These comments included, "I was listened to by the boys' parents." "Letting him and his parents hear what I have to say." "That mothers were there and could hear what the children did."

Victim wanted to understand offender's parents (n=4):

Some victims just wanted to know more about the offender's background and to understand what type of parents they had. These comments showed an increased awareness of what the offender's parents were really like, and lessened some preconceived generalizations about what kind of people raise kids that cause problems. "I had a chance to meet the offender's mother. She is deaf." "My attitude toward him improved. The more I though about this I wondered what sort of kid this was, running loose at 1:00 A.M. Where was his parents, do they care? My imagination was making me more angry about this. And when we met him and his mother, I changed my mind quite a bit. His mother was the type of person that could have been any one of my friends and she is just a woman trying to raise the kid by herself. And you can't be there every minute. She is doing the best she can."

Victim's Negative Themes

Dissatisfaction with the parental involvement seemed to be one of the most common responses by the victim. The victim's negative comments can't be easily lumped into one overall generalization, so the varied aspects are discussed in the context of smaller specific themes.

General dissatisfaction with parental involvement (n=14):

The victim's most common negative responses about parental involvement were of general dissatisfaction. This dissatisfaction was expressed in many ways, in the interviews before and after the mediation, including comments about anticipated unpleasantries as well as after the fact comments about an unpleasant experience. Comments included, "I think his parents will be the roughest." "Getting one father out of the meeting without trouble." "It's the parents who were the most difficult."

Offender's parents protect offender (n=11):

Some victims were dissatisfied with the manner in which the parent of the offender disrupted the mediation process by being overly protective of their child(ren). When this occurred, it was viewed in several ways—a hostile attitude of the parents; an interfering third party; and a weakness in the mediator's style. Victim's comments about overprotective parents included, "The offender's parent wouldn't let us kids mediate, he always had to be a part of it, and he got everybody mad." "They [Mediator] could have been more in control of the fathers." "I'd like to see the defendant come in without his parents who protect him."

Offender's parents hostile towards victim (n=11):

Several victims expressed concern about the offender's parents negative, hostile or uncooperative attitude shown during the mediation. "The mother was hostile in the meeting." However, several victims also expressed concern about anticipated hostile attitudes by the offender's parent, such as, "It kind of bothers me that this parents will be there and that there may be a confrontation with them." "That the mom will get upset and start threatening." Of the four victims who expressed such concern before the mediation, none of them expressed and similar concern after the mediation.

Offender's parents take responsibility for offender's actions (n=8):

Some victims expressed concern that the offenders were not being held accountable for their actions, and that the parents were accepting responsibility for their child's behavior. "Parents were not willing to make him take responsibility for his actions." "I don't want his dad to write a check for it, because that does nothing for the offender." "It [restitution] corresponds to what he can earn. We tried not to make it a burden on his mother." "To make sure that the juveniles answer for themselves and that the parents don't get too involved in it."

Offender's parents have poor parenting skills (n=7):

Some victims felt that poor parenting skills were linked to the offender's crime, especially providing inadequate guidance and support for the offender's growth and development. Such comments included, "The offender's dad gives him money and he doesn't know the value of it." "He was real happy with the restitution. The offender always wanted to have a job, but his dad wouldn't let him." "The offender was a victim of the society and her family. The society threw the girl into the fire. Her parents left her home alone while they were out of town, with alcohol in the house." "His parents never taught him right from wrong."

Offenders parents not present (n=7):

Some victims were disappointed that the offender's parents did not show up for the mediation. They expressed a loss for themselves in not being able to meet the offender's parents and also expressed concern that the offender's parents were not concerned enough to show up for the mediation. "I would have liked to have had a chance to talk with his parents." "I would have involved the mothers who were responsible for them." "One or both of the parents should have been there so they could have heard about what happened and the effect it has on others." "That the parents weren't even concerned enough to be there."

Offender Themes

Offender's responses for the open-ended questions, resulted in fewer and less elaborate comments that those stated by the victims. Therefore, it is difficult to ascertain, with any degree of certainty, the usefulness of the offender's comments. Listed below are three themes that emerged from the results.

Offenders didn't like their parents present (n=8):

Offenders stated several reasons why they did not like their parents present during the mediation process, including discomfort, fear of punishment and feeling overpowered by their parents. "I feel I am not being dealt with fairly. I am a minor, and my parents have made all the decisions. What I say is overruled. I wish I could have more to say about what I have to do."

Offenders uncomfortable meeting victim's parents (n=8):

Several of the offenders expressed discomfort or dissatisfaction with meeting the victim's parents because of the negative attitude or anger. "Between me and her it was friendly, but her parents were real mad." "Victim's mom wanted to know things, detail about the accident." "I don't think parents should be involved in mediation. They wanted out community service doubled."

Offenders liked meeting victim's parents (n=6):

Some of the offenders liked meeting the victim's parents and expressed satisfaction with the positive attitude of the victim's parents, satisfaction to talk with the victim's parents and a chance to understand what the victim's parents felt about the crime. "The victim's parents were nice to me." "That I got to talk to the victim's mother." "The victim and his parents felt a lot of pain."

CONCLUSION

Parental involvement does influence the mediation process, and parents attended over 50% of the mediation cases in this research project. There was a wide variation of attendance level at the program sites, from a low of 19% to a high of 82%. What influence parental involvement had on the mediation process was not examined in this research, although such research is needed considering the impact that parental involvement has on the mediation process.

The results presented are preliminary, and further research is needed to clarify and define the ramifications of parental involvement in the mediation process.

NOTE: This appendix was drafted by Boris Kalanj and Dale Jore.

Appendix 4: Case Study of Mediation in a Residential Burglary

"Crime Victims and Offenders in Mediation: An Emerging Area of Social Work Practice" *

Mark S. Umbreit, Ph.D.
School of Social Work
University of Minnesota

Interest among social workers and others in victim-offender mediation has been growing during the past decade. In 1978 there were a handful of programs, primarily in the Midwest. Today there are victim-offender mediation programs in nearly one hundred jurisdictions throughout the country (Umbreit, 1988), including major urban areas such as Miami and smaller communities such as Valparaiso (IN).

Programs continue to be primarily sponsored by private social service agencies working closely with the courts. A growing number of victim offender mediation programs, however, are being directly sponsored by probation departments or other public agencies. In this growing network, social workers are becoming active in many roles, including: community organizers; program developers; board members; trainers; and, either staff or volunteer mediators.

The rich heritage of social work practice in the juvenile and criminal justice systems dates back to the turn of the century when the juvenile court was established. The concept of victim-offender mediation, however, remains largely absent from social work literature. This article begins to build a bridge between social work practice in this emerging field and the social work literature. First, the basic purpose of this practice model will be presented. Next, the case management process will be identified. An actual case study of mediating conflict between a victim of home burglary and the offender will be offered. Finally, important issues related to program development and replication will be presented.

*Reprinted from *Social Work*, Volume 38, Number 1, January 1993 with permission from the National Association of Social Workers, Inc.

PURPOSE

Victim-offender mediation programs focus upon providing a conflict resolution process which is perceived as fair by both the victim and the offender (Umbreit, 1988, 1985). The mediator facilitates this process, by first allowing time to address informational and emotional needs, followed by a discussion of losses and the possibility of developing a mutually agreeable restitution obligation (i.e. money, work for the victim or the victim's choice of a charity, etc.).

Both crime victims and offenders are placed in a passive position by the criminal justice system, oftentimes not even receiving basic assistance or information. Victims often feel powerless and vulnerable. Some even feel twice victimized, first by the offender and then by an uncaring criminal justice system that doesn't have time for them. Offenders are rarely able to understand or be confronted with the human dimension of their criminal behavior, that victims are real people, not just objects to be abused. Offenders have many rationalizations for their behavior. It is not unusual for anger and frustration to be increase as the victim and offender move through the highly depersonalized justice process.

The victim-offender mediation process draws upon some rather old fashioned principles which recognize that crime is fundamentally against people, not just the State. Instead of placing the victim in a passive role and reinforcing an adversarial dynamic which often results in little emotional closure for the victim and little, if any, direct accountability by the offender to the victim, the mediation process facilitates active involvement by the victim in resolving the conflict.

MEDIATION PROCESS

There are four phases in the victim-offender mediation process (Umbreit, 1988): intake, preparation for mediation, mediation and follow-up. The intake phase begins with the court referral of offenders (most often those convicted of such crimes as theft and burglary). Most programs accept referrals after a formal admission of guilt has been entered with the court. Some programs accept cases that are referred prior to formal admission of guilt, as part of a deferred prosecution effort. Each case is assigned to a mediator.

The preparation for mediation phase begins when the mediator meets with both the offender and victim separately. During this individual session, the mediator listens to the story of each party, explains the program and encourages their participation. Mediators will usually meet first with the offender and, if he/she is willing to proceed with mediation, then later with the victim.

Encouragement of victim and offender participation in the mediation process must not be confused with coercion. The process is meant to be empowering for victims and offenders, presenting them with choices.

Following these separate meetings and the choice of both parties to participate, the mediator then initiates the mediation phase by scheduling a meeting. The mediation session begins with the mediator explaining his or her role, identifying the agenda, and stating communication ground rules. The first part of the meeting focuses upon a discussion of the facts and feelings related to the crime. Victims are given the rare opportunity to express their feeling directly to the person who violated them. They can get answers to questions such as "Why me?," or "How did you get into our house?," or "Were you stalking us and planning on coming back?." Victims are often relieved to finally see the offender, who usually bears little resemblance to the frightening character they had envisioned.

The mediation session places offenders in the uncomfortable position of having to face the person they violated. They are given the equally rare opportunity to display a more human dimension to their character, to even express remorse in a personal fashion. Through discussion of their feelings, both victim and offender have the opportunity to deal with each other as people, oftentimes from the same neighborhood, rather than as stereotypes and objects.

When the sharing of facts and feelings related to the crime is concluded, the second part of the meeting is then directed to discussion of losses and negotiation of a mutually acceptable restitution agreement as a tangible symbol of conflict resolution and a focal point for accountability. Mediators do not impose a restitution settlement. Joint victim-offender meetings usually last about one hour, with some meetings in the two hour range.

CASE STUDY

Anne and Bob's home was burglarized for the second time. They were furious. This was the second time their home had been burglarized. Both felt violated, as though they had been personally assaulted. Many questions went through their minds. Why was their house picked? Was it the same criminal that broke in several months ago? Were their movements being watched? Does someone have a personal vendetta against them?

Jim was picked up within several weeks of the burglary. He was twenty years old and had several minor brushes with the law as a juvenile but no prior adult convictions. Two months ago, Jim lost his job at a factory. He plead guilty to the charge.

During the sentencing hearing in court, as a condition of probation, he was referred to the Center for Victim Offender Mediation in Minneapolis, a program of the Minnesota Citizens Council on Crime and Justice. When first approached about the mediation program, Jim was not enthusiastic. During an individual meeting with Jim, the mediator explained to him that confronting his victim might be helpful for several reasons. First, he would have an opportunity to discuss what happened with the victim. Second, he would be able to negotiate a restitution agreement that was considered fair to both parties. Third, by taking such direct responsibility for his criminal behavior, he would also be able to have input into a portion of his court ordered punishment.

The mediator explained that while the court preferred his participation in this mediation program, he was not required to do so. If he felt that it was simply not appropriate for him, he could be referred back to the court to fulfill restitution through the normal procedures. He finally indicated that he would be willing to meet the victim and work out a way of paying them back.

After having secured Jim's willingness to try the mediation process, the mediator then met separately with Bob and Anne at their home. She first listened to their story about what happened. Both Bob and Anne expressed a great need to simply talk about how outraged they felt about this whole incident. In addition to feeling angry at the criminal who violated them, both indicated anger at the criminal justice system which seemed to treat them like a piece of evidence. They experienced another sense of victimization as a result of the rather insensitive manner in which the criminal justice system responded to their needs.

When there was finally time to explain the mediation program Bob and Anne were not interested initially. They couldn't see any value in confronting the offender. The mediator pointed out some possible benefits. They could let the offender know how angry they were and how this crime affected them. Many of the questions that Bob and Anne had asked the mediator, could be answered directly by the only person who really knew, the offender. Also, rather than sitting on the sidelines of the justice process, like most victims, Bob and Anne could get directly involved and help shape part of the penalty that their offender would be required to undergo by the court. Finally, both Bob and Anne would have the opportunity to negotiate a mutually acceptable restitution agreement that was considered fair to all parties.

After further thought, Bob and Anne agreed to try the mediation process. Both said that they were not certain of the value of such a confrontation but they certainly wanted to let that "punk " know how angry they were.

Because of the heightened level of anger involved in this case, co-mediators, both of whom were trained social work practitioners, were used. The mediation session was held at a neutral community center.

Several introductory comments were made by the lead mediator. She thanked participants for coming and trying the process. She clearly identified the purpose of the session: first, to provide time to talk about the burglary and how those involved felt about it, and second, to talk about losses and the possibility of negotiating a restitution agreement. The role of the mediators was explained. They were not official representatives of the court, nor could they impose any settlement on either party. Rather, their role was to provide an opportunity for both parties to talk about what happened and to see if a settlement could be reached. Whatever was agreed on, they emphasized, must be perceived as fair to both parties. The parties would first have some uninterrupted time to tell their stories.

The lead mediator asked Bob if he could tell Jim about what happened from his perspective and how it affected him. The hand movements of the mediator indicated that Bob was encouraged to talk directly to Jim. At this point, Bob had both arms rigidly crossed on his chest. He quickly began talking about how he was furious about this kind of "crap." He said he was fed up with kids who violated other people's property. Anne chose not to speak at this point.

Because of the level of anger expressed by Bob, the mediators were about to intervene to prevent any direct verbal attacks on Jim. Just before they intervened, however, something atypical occurred. Jim jumped out of his chair and said "I'm not taking this crap any longer—I've had it, I'm leaving." At that point, the co-mediator intervened by saying directly to Jim, "I'm sure this has been difficult listening to the anger expressed by Bob, but I know that he is interested in working out some kind of settlement. Could you just give it another ten minutes? If you can, I think we might be able to work something out tonight. If you want to leave after ten minutes, it's up to you." Jim paused and then sat down.

The comment of the co-mediator appeared to have validated some of Jim's concern that he was being "dumped upon." From this point on, Bob's communication to Jim was far less emotional and his body language slowly began to loosen up.

When it became evident that Bob and Anne had completed their initial statement, the mediator then turned to Jim and asked him if he could tell them what happened from his perspective. Jim explained how he was out drinking with some buddies and they needed extra money. They were cruising around in the neighborhood and saw what appeared to be an empty house, no lights were on. They knocked on the front door and, since no one responded, walked around the house and broke in through the back door. Once in the house, they had taken a television, VCR, stereo set and some loose cash amounting to about $100. Jim explained how they had not initially intended to break into Bob and Anne's home. When they did break in, he was quite nervous and anxious to get out of the home as quick as possible. Jim clearly admitted that he took the items mentioned above.

After Jim completed his version of what happened, Bob and Anne asked Jim numerous questions. Why us? Were you watching our movements? Jim again indicated that he had not been watching them. Anne then asked Jim if he knew their daughter Carol. Jim said he did. She mentioned that Carol had been living on the streets for the past year ever since she had left a drug treatment center. Jim said he knew that. Bob asked Jim when he saw Carol again if he would mention that her mom and dad loved her and would welcome her home if she would be willing to come back.

It was clear at this time that the conflict had been reframed; rather than interacting in stereotypic roles of "victim" and "offender," the participants now interacted at a more human level, with concern about issues beyond the criminal event.

Discussion of what happened that evening and how all parties felt about it lasted for nearly one hour. Before the co-mediator suggested discussing restitution, some time of silence was allowed to give both parties an opportunity to raise any additional questions.

The co-mediator then stated that it was now time to review the losses that Bob and Anne had incurred and to begin the process of negotiating a restitution agreement if that was possible. The mediator turned to Anne and asked her to identify the losses they incurred, including providing any documentation. Anne presented a long list of items. Jim was then asked to review this list and comment.

Jim had a number of questions about several items and particularly their replacement value. After discussing this further with Anne and Bob, he indicated that he now understood the full impact of what he did and was ready to talk about a plan to "make things right."

Bob, Anne, and Jim worked out a restitution plan that required Jim to pay $50 a month over a ten month period, beginning next month. The terms of the restitution agreement were read back to both parties prior to writing them up in an agreement. When the agreement was written, both parties signed it and copies were given to each. A copy would also be forwarded to Jim's probation officer.

The co-mediator then stated that "in cases like this when an agreement is reached, we prefer that both parties meet briefly several months from now to check out how the agreement is working out. What do you think about doing this?" Jim turned to Bob and Anne and said "I'd really like to do that...could we have it at my house?." He added, "I would like you to meet my wife and my baby...I'm not a criminal." The meeting was scheduled two months later at Jim's home, with a mediator present. Jim offered to cook lasagna. Bob and Anne quickly indicated their interest.

REFLECTION ON THE CASE STUDY

The initial anger and hostility of the victims toward the offender was later transformed into a human understanding of each other and a specific plan for "making things right." This transformation had little to do with the amount of information and advice provided by the mediators (which was minimal) during the mediation session. Rather, the process of reconciliation had far more to do with the safe structure provided by the mediators that allowed the parties to deal directly with each other.

The two mediators talked at most 15-20% of the time, and the disputants 80-85% of the time. Mediators were more verbally active at three points in the process. First, during the opening statement, the mediators explained their role, identified ground rules and the agenda, and initiated direct victim-offender communication. The mediators then faded into the background. Midway into the session, a clear transition point was required to move from talking about what happened and how they felt to then discussing the need for restitution. The mediators again faded more into the background. Finally, when efforts were being made to work out a written agreement, the mediators needed to be more active in presenting various options and helping the parties structure the agreement in a way that was workable.

The mediators in this case employed an empowering, or non-directive, style of mediation (Umbreit, 1988). Experience in the field of victim-offender mediation has found that an empowering, rather than controlling, style is often far more effective in addressing the emotional needs of the parties, as well as securing workable restitution plans.

The experience of the Bob, Anne, and Jim illustrates the purpose of the victim-offender mediation process. Consistent with a growing body of research (Coates and Gehm, 1989; Davis et. al., 1980; Marshall and Merry, 1990; Umbreit, 1989,1990; Wright and Galaway, 1988), Bob, Anne, and Jim felt the mediation process and outcome was fair. All were very satisfied with participation in the program. Rather than playing passive roles in the resolution of the conflict between them, Bob, Anne, and Jim actively participated in "making things right." During a subsequent conversation with Bob he commented that "this was the first time (after several victimizations) that I ever felt any sense of fairness. The courts always ignored me before. They didn't care about my concerns. And Jim wasn't such a bad kid after all, was he?" Jim also indicated that he felt better after the mediation and more aware of the impact the burglary had on the Bob and Anne.

DEVELOPMENT AND REPLICATION ISSUES

As a growing number of communities consider developing a victim-offender mediation program, a number of important issues should be considered. Building of public and system support for the new program will be crucial. Experience in many communities has indicated that although some criminal justice officials may be initially skeptical (most notably prosecutors, judges and victim advocates) their support usually can be obtained. Once they learn more about the mediation process and how it affects both victims and offenders, they usually become supportive, or even active, in developing the new program.

The most likely referral sources will be judges and probation staff. Prosecutors, defense attorneys and victim assistance staff can also be effective referral sources.

Identifying an appropriate group of victims and offenders to work with is vital. Experience in thousands of mediation cases over the past ten years has shown that the program is effective with non-violent property offenses such as vandalism, theft and burglary. Most offenders are either first or second time law violators. Contrary to other types of mediation, most (but not all) victims and offenders had no prior relationship.

Many programs also work with assault cases. A few programs are beginning to work with more violent crime such as armed robbery, sexual assault and attempted homicide. In fact, it has often been victims of violent crime that have advocated extending the mediation process to more serious cases. However, this does not include domestic assault. The mediation process has been effective in assisting victims of violent crime in regaining a sense of power and control in their lives, as well as the ability to "let go" of the victimization experience (Umbreit, 1988). However, mediation for a violent crime requires a far more intense process, and is not recommended for new programs.

Those interested in developing a program need to decide early whether to work with either juvenile and/or adult offenders. Since the juvenile and adult systems are entirely different, working with both will require more initial development time.

Working collaboratively with existing victims' services programs, as well as offender treatment programs, is important. Although the victim-offender mediation process has been found to offer a number of benefits to both parties, the process also has limitations. Many victims and offenders are in need of more extensive services than can be offered through the mediation process. At best, the mediation process is part of a larger response to the needs facing crime victims and their offenders.

Securing resources to operate a new victim-offender mediation program is critical. In most communities, a small staff that supervises a larger pool of trained volunteer mediators is sufficient. This keeps the program's costs down and, more importantly, empowers citizens to become directly involved in resolving criminal conflict in their communities. The provision of 25-30 hours of effective mediation training and continued in-service training is important.

Replication of the victim-offender mediation model requires effective community organizing and program development skills. Most importantly, it requires a deep commitment to restorative principles of justice that empower crime victims and their offenders to resolve their conflict and to let go of the victimization experience.

REFERENCES

Coates, Robert B. and Gehm, John (1989). "An Empirical Assessment." In Martin Wright and Burt Galaway (eds.) *Mediation and Criminal Justice.* London: Sage.

Davis, Robert et. al. (1980). *Mediation and Arbitration as Alternative to Prosecution in Felony Arrest Cases: An Evaluation of the Brooklyn Dispute Resolution Center.* New York, NY: Vera Institute of Justice.

Marshall, Tony and Merry, Susan (1990). *Crime and Accountability: Victim Offender Mediation in Practice.* London: Home Office.

Umbreit, Mark S. (1990). "Fairness and Victims of Burglary." In: Burt Galaway and Joe Hudson (eds.), *Criminal Justice, Restitution and Reconciliation*

Umbreit, Mark S. (1989). "Crime Victims Seeking Fairness, Not Revenge." *Federal Probation,* 93(3), 52-57.

Umbreit, Mark S. (1988). "Mediation of Victim Offender Conflict." *Missouri Journal of Dispute Resolution,* 85-105.

Umbreit, Mark S. (1988). "Violent Offenders and Their Victims." In: Martin Wright and Burt Galaway (eds.). *Mediation and Criminal Justice.* London: Sage.

Umbreit, Mark S. (1985). *Crime and Reconciliation: Creative Options for Victims and Offenders.* Nashville: Abingdon.

Wright, Martin and Galaway, Burt (1988). *Mediation and Criminal Justice.* London: Sage.

A special thanks is due to Mary Pat Maher, M.S.W., who served as the lead mediator in this case, and to the Minnesota Citizens Council on Crime and Justice, which had the vision to develop a program involving victim-offender mediation and reconciliation.

Appendix 5. Stakeholder Analysis Form

PERSON/TITLE	LEVEL OF SUPPORT	WHO CAN INFLUENCE THEM	STRATEGY

Appendix 6. Sample Victim Information Letter

Dear _____ :

You may be interested in the Victim-Offender Mediation Program.

It can provide a unique opportunity for victims of crime to:

° receive answers to questions about the offense that only the offender can provide;

• express your frustration and concerns directly to the person who should hear them—the offender;

• become directly involved in the sentence your offender receives, rather than sitting on the sidelines;

• determine the amount and form of restitution to cover your losses through a structured meeting with the offender, in the presence of a trained mediator.

While the Victim-Offender Mediation Program is neither appropriate for all victims nor a cure-all for crime in our communities, many victims have found it beneficial. As a victim, participation is totally your choice.

We encourage you to at least learn more about the possible benefits of the program and then make your decision.

Should you be interested, the following staff person (or volunteer) will be contacting you: _____ .

Note to Program Staff:
Be aware that the word "reconciliation" can push buttons and irritate some victims and many victim advocates.

Appendix 7. Program Evaluation Kit: Victim-Offender Mediation Programs

Prepared by:

Mark S. Umbreit, Ph.D.
Principal Investigator
Citizens Council Mediation Services
Minnesota Citizens Council on Crime and Justice
822 South Third St., Minneapolis, MN 55415

School of Social Work
University of Minnesota
400 Ford Hall, Minneapolis, MN 55455

July 1992

This Program Evaluation Kit was made possible by a grant from the State Justice Institute in Alexandria, VA to the Minnesota Citizens Council on Crime and Justice in Minneapolis, which has granted permission for its reproduction in this volume. The Minnesota Citizens Council on Crime and Justice contracted with the University of Minnesota for the services of the Principal Investigator.

Use of the questionnaires should give credit in the following manner: "The questionnaires used by our program are based on those initially prepared by Dr. Mark Umbreit of the School of Social Work, University of Minnesota. Dr. Umbreit served as the principal investigator for the Citizens Council Mediation Services in Minneapolis in connection with a study of victim-offender mediation programs in four states. This research was funded by the State Justice Institute in Alexandria, VA through a grant to the Minnesota Citizens Council on Crime and Justice, Mediation Services. These questionnaires were adapted from the larger study conducted by Dr. Umbreit."

INTRODUCTION

Victim-offender mediation and reconciliation programs provide an opportunity for those who commit criminal offenses to meet face-to-face with the person they victimized, in the presence of a trained mediator. The programs are based on a conflict resolution process that is designed to be fair to both parties. The competency of the mediator is the most critical factor related to whether the parties have their informational, emotional and material needs met by the mediation process.

Consumer feedback about any type of service provision, including mediation, is an important element in maintaining quality control. Through a consistent and reliable system of receiving feedback from clients about their satisfaction with the mediation process and outcomes, important and helpful information can be obtained for program managers and mediators.

This Program Evaluation Kit is designed to be a self-administered system for routinely evaluating client satisfaction as part of the ongoing operation of a victim-offender mediation program. By "self-administered" we mean that this evaluation kit can be implemented by program staff and volunteers, without the need for a special program evaluation grant or connection with a researcher at a university or related institution. If used properly, the program evaluation system presented can be easily integrated into the ongoing operation of the program and can offer a good, quality experience for participants by asking for feedback about how their case was handled.

The Program Evaluation Kit has been developed from the knowledge and experience gained from a two-and-half-year, multi-state evaluation of victim-offender mediation programs working with juvenile offenders and their victims. This research, which represented the largest study of victim-offender mediation in the U.S., was completed during the summer of 1992. It was funded by a grant from the State Justice Institute in Alexandria, VA to the Minnesota Citizens Council on Crime and Justice in Minneapolis. The Citizens Council contracted with Dr. Mark Umbreit at the School of Social Work, the University of Minnesota, to serve as principal investigator.

The questionnaires included in this Program Evaluation Kit represent a collapsed version of the larger instruments developed and administered by Dr. Umbreit and his staff in a total of 1,153 interviews with victims and offenders related to mediation programs in Albuquerque (NM), Austin (TX), Minneapolis (MN) and Oakland (CA). With slight modification, the enclosed questionnaires can be used for either juvenile or adult offenders.

QUESTIONNAIRES

Both mediation participants and a comparison group, available to all mediation programs and consisting of those victims and offenders who are referred to mediation but who do not participate, should be interviewed using the following instruments:

(Mediation Groups)
1. Victim post-mediation questionnaire
2. Offender post-mediation questionnaire

(Comparison Groups)
3. Victim referred-but-no-mediation questionnaire
4. Offender referred-but-no-mediation questionnaire

ANSWERS TO IMPORTANT QUESTIONS

Who Should Conduct the Interviews?

It is important that persons with a stake in the outcome of the mediation not do the interviewing. For example, the mediator in the case should not conduct the interview. The best arrangement is to have either a volunteer (who does not currently serve as a mediator) or a student intern conduct the interviews. Whoever does the interviewing should practice and role-play their interviewing skills, under supervision, prior to doing the actual interviewing with victims and offenders.

How Are Interviews Administered?

All of the questionnaires are designed to be administered during a telephone interview, which should take 15 to 30 minutes.

When Should the Post-Mediation Interviews Occur?

Post-mediation interviews with victims and offenders should occur approximately two months after the date of the mediation.

When Should the Comparison-Group Interviews Occur?

Interviews with victims and offenders who were referred to the program but who did not participate in mediation should be interviewed approximately two months after the date their case receives a disposition from the court, or the date in which the mediation program refers the case back to the court. The main issue is that the two-month period be measured from the same starting point in all cases.

Should a Random Sample of Cases be Selected for Interviews?

Many victim-offender mediation programs do not have a large enough base of case referrals to allow for random sampling of cases for interviews. In these programs, an availability sample should be used. This simply means that all available subjects are given the opportunity to be interviewed.

For those programs with a large and consistent base of case referrals, however, a systematic random sample is far more desirable. A systematic random sample simply means randomly selecting a starting point in a list of cases, and then selecting every other case to be interviewed.

Must Interviews be Conducted with the Comparison Groups?

Interviewing those victims and offenders who were referred to the program but who did not participate in mediation will provide an important point of comparison. For example, a finding that 90% of victims in mediation are satisfied with the way their case was handled by the justice system, including the mediation process, is impressive. Without a comparison group, however, it is unclear whether 90% of similar victims who did not participate in mediation were also satisfied with the way their case was handled by the justice system.

While it is clearly preferable to interview victims and offenders in the mediation program, as well as those who were referred but did not participate, this is not absolutely required. If limited resources require fewer interviews, then simply interviewing those in mediation is acceptable. This is a weaker and less valid technique for evaluating the program, yet data on program participants alone is better than no evaluation data at all.

It should be noted that a stronger comparison group would consist of offenders from the same jurisdiction who are matched with mediation offenders along the variable of age, sex, race, offense and prior convictions, as well as the victims of these matched offenders. This type of comparison group, however, is more difficult to obtain and would require the assistance of a person trained in research techniques and program evaluation.

What If Additional Questions Need to be Asked?

There is no reason why additional questions that relate to the needs of a specific program cannot be asked. In fact, this is encouraged. The more practical and relevant the system of program evaluation, the more likely that it will be made use of as part of the ongoing operation of the program.

POST-MEDIATION VICTIM INTERVIEW SCHEDULE

Program Site: _____

Program Case Number: _____

Interview Date:_____

Interviewer: _____

Age of victim: ____

Gender: ____

Race: ____

Mark Umbreit, Ph.D.
Principal Investigator
Citizens Council Mediation Services
Minnesota Citizens Council on Crime and Justice

School of Social Work
University of Minnesota

July 1992

POST-MEDIATION VICTIM INTERVIEW SCHEDULE

I WOULD LIKE TO BEGIN BY ASKING YOU A FEW GENERAL QUES-
TIONS.

1. Did you know the offender before the crime occurred?

           a. yes   b. no

  1A. IF YES: How did you know the offender?

          a. friend

          b. acquaintance

          c. neighbor

          d. other _____

2. Have you been a victim of a crime before?

           a. yes   b. no

  2A. IF YES: How many prior victimizations? ___

    What kind of crime were they?

          a. crimes against property ___ (no.)

          b. crimes against person ___ (no.)

3. Of the following possible effects of the crime on your life, which was
the most important effect for you?

          a. a greater sense of fear

          b. the loss of property

          c. the damage to property

          d. the hassle of dealing with police and court officials

          e. a feeling of powerlessness

I WOULD NOW LIKE TO ASK YOU A FEW QUESTIONS ABOUT YOUR
EXPERIENCE WITH THE JUSTICE SYSTEM IN THIS CASE.

4. How satisfied were you with the way the justice
system handled your case?

          a. very satisfied

          b. satisfied

          c. dissatisfied

          d. very dissatisfied

5. Do you believe that your opinion regarding the crime and offender was adequately considered in this case?

a. yes   b. no

6. Were you informed by the juvenile justice system as to the action taken regarding the offender in your case?

a. yes   b. no

7. Do you believe the offender was adequately held accountable for his/her behavior?

a. yes   b. no

8. Do you believe that the victim-offender mediation program should be a standard part of the criminal justice system and offered, on a voluntary basis, to all victims who would find it helpful?

a. yes   b. no

NOW I WOULD LIKE TO ASK A FEW QUESTIONS ABOUT THE VICTIM-OFFENDER MEDIATION PROGRAM.

9. Do you feel that you're being in the mediation program was your own choice?

a. yes   b. no

9A. IF YES: Why did you chose to participate in the victim-offender mediation program?

a. to get paid back for losses

b. to let the offender know how I felt about the crime

c. to receive answers to questions I had

d. to help the offender

e. to receive an apology

f. other _____

10. Do you feel the mediator prepared you sufficiently for the meeting with your offender?

a. yes   b. no

10A. What was the most helpful in this preparation for mediation? (select one)

a. being told what happens in mediation

b. having someone listen to my story about what hap⟩

c. explaining what the possible benefits of mediation ⟨

d. other _____

10B. What was the least helpful in this preparation for mediation? (select one)

a. not receiving enough information about mediation

b. feeling that you had no choice about participation in mediation

c. no one listened to your story about what happened or how you felt about it

d. you never understood why mediation could be of benefit to you

11. Who was present at the mediation session? [INTERVIEWER NOTE: roles, not names]

a. number of mediators ___

b. number of victims ___

c. number of people with victim ___

d. number of offenders ___

e. number of people with offender ___

12. How long did the mediation session last?_____

13. Would you say the tone of the meeting was generally

a. friendly

b. hostile

c. other _____

14. Were you surprised by anything that occurred in the mediation session?

a. yes   b. no

14A. IF YES: By what?

a. it went better than you expected

b. it was worse than you expected

c. the offender seemed sincere

d. the offender was arrogant

e. other _____

NOW I WOULD LIKE TO ASK YOU SOME QUESTIONS ABOUT YOUR EXPERIENCE IN THE MEETING WITH THE OFFENDER. FOR EACH OF THE FOLLOWING ITEMS, PLEASE TELL ME WHETHER THE ITEM IS VERY IMPORTANT, IMPORTANT, UNIMPORTANT, OR VERY UNIMPORTANT.

15. To receive answers to questions you would like to ask the offender.

      a. very important

      b. important

      c. unimportant

      d. very unimportant

15A. What are your thoughts about this?

16. To tell the offender how the crime affected you.

      a. very important

      b. important

      c. unimportant

      d. very unimportant

16A. Why do you say that?

17. To get paid back for your losses by the offender.

      a. very important

      b. important

      c. unimportant

      d. very unimportant

17A. Please tell me more about this.

18. That the offender gets some counseling or other type of help.

      a. very important

      b. important

      c. unimportant

      d. very unimportant

18A. Why is that?

19. To have the offender committed to a correctional institution.

    a. very important

    b. important

    c. unimportant

    d. very unimportant

19A. Could you tell me more about this?

20. To have the offender say he or she is sorry.

    a. very important

    b. important

    c. unimportant

    d. very unimportant

20A. Did the offender seem to be sorry about the way he/she hurt you?

    a. yes   b. no

20B. Did the offender offer an apology?

    a. yes   b.no

21. To have the opportunity to negotiate a pay-back agreement with the offender that was acceptable to both of you.

    a. very important

    b. important

    c. unimportant

    d. very unimportant

21A. Why is that?

I WOULD LIKE TO ASK YOU SOME ADDITIONAL QUESTIONS ABOUT THE MEETING WITH THE OFFENDER AND ITS OUTCOME.

22. Was a pay-back agreement negotiated during the mediation session with the offender?

    a. yes   b. no

22A. IF YES: What was agreed upon?

        a. amount of money ___

        b. amount of work ___

        c. other _____

23. Was the restitution agreement fair to you?

        a. yes   b. no

23A. Could you tell me more about this?

24. Was the restitution agreement fair to the offender?

        a. yes   b. no

24A. Why do you say that?

25. Was it helpful to meet the offender?

        a. not at all helpful

        b. somewhat helpful

        c. very helpful

25A. Why?

26. Which of the following choices best describes your attitude toward the offender at this point in time?

        a. very positive

        b. positive

        c. mixed: positive and negative

        d. negative

        e. very negative

27. Are you afraid the offender will commit another crime against you?

        a. yes   b. no

28. How do you now feel about the crime committed against you?

        a. very upset

        b. somewhat upset

        c. not upset

29. How likely do you think it is that the offender will commit another crime against somebody?

        a. very likely

        b. likely

        c. unlikely

        d. very unlikely

30. Which of these choices best describes your attitude about the mediation session with your offender:

        a. very positive

        b. positive

        c. mixed: positive and negative

        d. negative

        e. very negative

30A. What are your thoughts about this?

31. Who did most of the talking during the mediation session? (roles, not names)

        a. the mediator

        b. yourself, as the victim

        c. the offender

32. Of the following items, please rank the three most important tasks of the mediator, with #1 being the most important.

rank

_____ a. providing leadership in the meeting

_____ b. making me and the offender feel comfortable and safe

_____ c. taking charge and doing most of the talking

_____ d. allowing plenty of time for me to talk directly with the offender

_____ e. being a good listener

_____ f. helping formulate the restitution agreement

_____ g. other _____

33. Do you believe the mediator was fair?

        a. yes   b. no

33A. IF NO: In what way was he or she unfair?

34. Which of these choices best describes your attitude about the mediator who worked with you and the offender:

   a. very satisfied

   b. satisfied

   c. no attitude

   d. dissatisfied

   e. very dissatisfied

34A. Could you explain your answer?

35. If you had it to do over again, would you again choose to meet the offender with a mediator?

   a. yes   b. no

35A. What are your thoughts about this?

36. Would you recommend victim-offender mediation to other victims of crime?

   a. yes   b. no

36A. Could you explain your answer?

37. When you left the mediation session with your offender, how satisfied were you about the outcome of the meeting?

   a. very satisfied

   b. satisfied

   c. dissatisfied

   d. very dissatisfied

38. What three things did you find the most satisfying about the victim-offender mediation experience?

   1. _____

   2. _____

3. _____

39. What three things did you find least satisfying about the victim-of-fender mediation experience?

1. _____

2. _____

3. _____

THE FOLLOWING REPRESENT STATEMENTS THAT ARE SOMETIMES MADE BY VICTIMS WHO PARTICIPATE IN VICTIM-OFFENDER MEDIATION. PLEASE INDICATE WHETHER YOU STRONGLY AGREE, AGREE, DISAGREE OR STRONGLY DISAGREE WITH EACH STATEMENT.

	STRONGLY AGREE	AGREE	DISAGREE	STRONGLY DISAGREE
40. Victim-offender mediation allowed me to express my feelings about being victimized.				
41. Victim-offender mediation allowed me to participate more fully in the criminal justice process.				
42. The offender was not sincere in his/her participation.				

	STRONGLY AGREE	AGREE	DISAGREE	STRONGLY DISAGREE
43. I have a better understanding of why the crime was committed against me.				
44. The offender participated only because he/she was trying to stay out of jail.				
45. Participation in victim-offender mediation made the criminal justice process more responsive to my needs as a human being.				

46. As a result of your participation in victim-offender mediation, have any of your attitudes about crime or the juvenile justice system changed?

    a. yes b. no

    46A. IF YES: What attitudes and why?

47. Of the following items, please rank the three most important concerns you have related to fairness in the justice system, with #1 being the most important.

rank

___ a. punishing the offender

___ b. paying back the victim

___ c. getting help for the offender

___ d. actively participating in the juvenile justice system

___ e. receiving the offender's expression of apology

___ f. other _____

48. Given your understanding of fairness, did you experience fairness within the justice system in your case?

     a. yes   b. no

49. Is there anything else you would like to say about the mediation session with your offender or about how your case was handled?

THANK YOU VERY MUCH FOR YOUR WILLINGNESS TO PARTICIPATE IN THIS PROGRAM EVALUATION.

REFERRED-BUT-NO-MEDIATION VICTIM INTERVIEW SCHEDULE

Program Site: _____

Program Case Number: _____

Interview Date:_____

Interviewer: _____

Age of victim: ____

Gender: ____

Race: ____

Mark Umbreit, Ph.D.
Principal Investigator
Citizens Council Mediation Services
Minnesota Citizens Council on Crime and Justice

School of Social Work
University of Minnesota

July 1992

REFERRED-BUT-NO-MEDIATION VICTIM
INTERVIEW SCHEDULE

I WOULD FIRST LIKE TO ASK YOU A FEW QUESTIONS ABOUT YOUR
EXPERIENCE WITH THE JUSTICE SYSTEM IN THIS CASE.

1. How satisfied were you with the way the justice system handled your
   case?

   a. very satisfied

   b. satisfied

   c. dissatisfied

   d. very dissatisfied

2. Do you believe that your opinion regarding the crime and offender
   was adequately considered in this case?

   a. yes   b. no

3. Were you informed by the juvenile justice system as to the action
   taken regarding the offender in your case?

   a. yes   b. no

4. Do you believe the offender was adequately held accountable for
   his/her behavior?

   a. yes   b. no

5. Do you believe that a victim-offender mediation program should be a
   standard part of the criminal justice system and offered, on a voluntary basis, to all victims who would find it helpful?

   a. yes   b. no

6. Clearly, victim-offender mediation is not something everyone wants
   to participate in. Can you tell me why you chose not to participate?

7. Is there anything that might have made it easier or more tempting to
   participate in the victim offender mediation program?

FOR EACH OF THE FOLLOWING ITEMS, PLEASE TELL ME WHETHER THE ITEM IS VERY IMPORTANT, IMPORTANT, UNIMPORTANT OR VERY UNIMPORTANT.

8. To receive answers to questions you would like to ask the offender.
   - a. very important
   - b. important
   - c. unimportant
   - d. very unimportant

9. To tell the offender how the crime affected you.
   - a. very important
   - b. important
   - c. unimportant
   - d. very unimportant

10. To get paid back for your losses by the offender.
   - a. very important
   - b. important
   - c. unimportant
   - d. very unimportant

11. That the offender gets some counseling or other type of help.
   - a. very important
   - b. important
   - c. unimportant
   - d. very unimportant

12. To have the offender committed to a correctional institution.
   - a. very important
   - b. important
   - c. unimportant
   - d. very unimportant

13. To have the offender say he or she is sorry.
   - a. very important
   - b. important
   - c. unimportant
   - d. very unimportant

14. To have the opportunity to work out a pay-back agreement with the offender that is acceptable to both of you.

>   a. very important
>
>   b. important
>
>   c. unimportant
>
>   d. very unimportant

15. Do you think that a meeting with the offender might be helpful?

>   a. not at all helpful
>
>   b. somewhat helpful
>
>   c. very helpful

16. Which of the following choices best describes your attitude toward the offender at this point in time?

>   a. very positive
>
>   b. positive
>
>   c. mixed: positive and negative
>
>   d. negative
>
>   e. very negative

17. Which of the following choices best describes your attitude toward the idea of meeting your offender, even though you did not participate in the victim-offender mediation program?

>   a. very positive
>
>   b. positive
>
>   c. mixed: positive and negative
>
>   d. negative
>
>   e. very negative

18. Are you afraid the offender will commit another crime against you?

>   a. yes   n. no

19. How do you now feel about the crime committed against you?

>   a. very upset
>
>   b. somewhat upset
>
>   c. not upset

WE ARE ALMOST DONE, BUT BEFORE ENDING I WOULD LIKE TO ASK YOU A COUPLE QUESTIONS ABOUT FAIRNESS.

20. Of the following items, which is the most important to your thinking about fairness in the justice system?

         a. punishing the offender

         b. paying back the victim

         c. getting help for the offender

         d. actively participating in the juvenile justice system

         e. receiving the offender's expression of apology

21. Given your understanding of fairness, did you experience fairness within the justice system in your case?

         a. yes   b. no

THIS COMPLETES OUR FORMAL INTERVIEW.

22. Is there anything else you would like to say about how the justice system handled your case?

THANK YOU VERY MUCH FOR PARTICIPATING IN THIS PROGRAM EVALUATION.

POST-MEDIATION OFFENDER INTERVIEW SCHEDULE

Program Site: _____

Program Case Number: _____

Interview Date:_____

Interviewer: _____

Age of offender: ____

Gender: ____

Race: ____

Offense: _____

.

Mark Umbreit, Ph.D.
Principal Investigator
Citizens Council Mediation Services
Minnesota Citizens Council on Crime and Justice

School of Social Work
University of Minnesota

July 1992

POST-MEDIATION OFFENDER INTERVIEW SCHEDULE

FIRST, I WOULD LIKE TO ASK YOU A COUPLE OF QUESTIONS ABOUT
YOUR EXPERIENCE WITH THE JUSTICE SYSTEM IN THIS CASE.

1. How satisfied were you with the way the justice system handled your
   case?

         a. very satisfied

         b. satisfied

         c. dissatisfied

         d. very dissatisfied

2. Do you believe you were adequately held accountable for the crime
   you committed?

         a. yes   b. no

NOW I WOULD LIKE TO ASK A FEW QUESTIONS ABOUT THE VIC-
TIM-OFFENDER MEDIATION PROGRAM.

3. Do you feel that you're being in the mediation program was your own
   choice?

         a. yes   b. no

   3A. IF YES: Why did you chose to participate in the victim-offender
mediation program?

         a. to pay back the victim for their losses

         b. to let the victim know why I did it

         c. to offer an apology

         d. to take direct responsibility for making things right

         e. other _____

4. Do you feel the mediator prepared you sufficiently for the meeting
   with your offender?

         a. yes   b. no

   4A. What was the most helpful in this preparation for mediation? (select one)

         a. being told what happens in mediation

         b. having someone listen to my story about what happe

         c. explaining what the possible benefits of mediation a

         d. other _____

4B. What was the least helpful in this preparation for mediation? (select one)

> a. not receiving enough information about mediation
>
> b. feeling that you had no choice about participation in mediation
>
> c. no one listened to your story about what happened or how you felt about it
>
> d. you never understood why mediation could be of benefit to you

5. Who was present at the mediation session?

[INTERVIEWER NOTE: roles, not names]

> a. number of mediators ___
>
> b. number of victims ___
>
> c. number of people with victim ___
>
> d. number of offenders ___
>
> e. number of people with offender ___

6. How long did the mediation session last?_____

7. Would you say the tone of the meeting was generally

> a. friendly
>
> b. hostile
>
> c. other _____

7A. Could you tell me more about this?

8. Were you surprised by anything that occurred in the mediation session?

> a. yes   b. no

8A. IF YES: By what?

> a. it went better than you expected
>
> b. it was worse than you expected
>
> c. the victim seemed to care about me
>
> d. the victim was so angry
>
> e. other _____

NOW I WOULD LIKE TO ASK YOU SOME QUESTIONS ABOUT YOUR EXPERIENCE IN THE MEETING WITH THE VICTIM. FOR EACH OF THE

FOLLOWING ITEMS, PLEASE TELL ME WHETHER THE ITEM IS VERY IMPORTANT, IMPORTANT, UNIMPORTANT OR VERY UNIMPORTANT.

9. To be able to tell the victim what happened.

> a. very important
>
> b. important
>
> c. unimportant
>
> d. very unimportant

9A. What are your thoughts about this?

10. To pay back the victim by paying them money or doing some work.

> a. very important
>
> b. important
>
> c. unimportant
>
> d. very unimportant

10A. Please tell me more about this.

11. To have the opportunity to work out a pay-back agreement with the victim that was acceptable to both of you.

> a. very important
>
> b. important
>
> c. unimportant
>
> d. very unimportant

11A. What's your thinking behind this?

12. To be able to apologize to the victim for what you did.

> a. very important
>
> b. important
>
> c. unimportant
>
> d. very unimportant

12A. Did you apologize to your victim?

> a. yes   b. no

12B. Could you tell me more about this?

I WOULD LIKE TO ASK YOU SOME ADDITIONAL QUESTIONS ABOUT
THE MEETING WITH THE VICTIM AND ITS OUTCOME.

13. Was a pay-back agreement negotiated during the mediation session
    with the victim?

                        a. yes   b. no
    13A. IF YES: What was agreed upon?

                        a. amount of money ___

                        b. amount of work ___

                        c. other _____

14. Was the restitution agreement fair to you?

                        a. yes   b. no
    14A. Could you tell me more about this?

15. Was the restitution agreement fair to the victim?

                        a. yes   b. no

    15A. Why do you say that?

16. Was it helpful to meet the victim?

                        a. not at all helpful

                        b. somewhat helpful

                        c. very helpful
    16A. Why?

17. Do you feel better after having met with the victim?

                        a. yes   b. no
    17A. What are your thoughts about this?

18. Which of the following choices best describes your attitude toward
    the victim at this point in time?

                        a. very positive

b. positive

c. mixed: positive and negative

d. negative

e. very negative

19. Do you think the victim had a better opinion of you after you met with each other?

a. yes   b. no

19A. Why is that?

20. How likely do you think it is that you will complete the agreement to pay back the victim?

a. very likely

b. likely

c. unlikely

d. very unlikely

20A. Why do you say that?

21. How likely do you think it is that you will commit another crime?

a. very likely

b. likely

c. unlikely

d. very unlikely

21A. Why do you say that?

22. Which of these choices best describes your attitude about the mediation session with your victim?

a. very positive

b. positive

c. mixed: positive and negative

d. negative

e. very negative

22A. What are your thoughts about this?

23. Who did most of the talking during the mediation session? (roles, not names)

        a. the mediator

        b. yourself, as the victim

        c. the offender

24. Of the following items, please rank the three most important tasks of the mediator, with #1 being the most important.

rank

____   a. providing leadership in the meeting

____   b. making me and the victim feel comfortable and safe

____   c. taking charge and doing most of the talking

____   d. allowing plenty of time for me to talk directly with the victim

____   e. being a good listener

____   f. helping us formulate the restitution agreement

____   g. other _____

25. Do you believe the mediator was fair?

        a. yes   b. no

25A. IF NO: In what way was he or she unfair?

26. Which of these choices best describes your attitude about the mediator who worked with you and the victim:

        a. very satisfied

        b. satisfied

        c. no attitude

        d. dissatisfied

        e. very dissatisfied

26A. Could you explain your answer?

27. If you had it to do over again, would you again choose to meet the victim with a mediator?

        a. yes   b. no

27A. What are your thoughts about this?

28. Would you recommend victim-offender mediation to other friends that might get in trouble?

                    a. yes   b. no
  28a. Could you explain your answer?

29. When you left the mediation session with your victim, how satisfied were you about the outcome of the meeting?

                    a. very satisfied
                    b. satisfied
                    c. dissatisfied
                    d. very dissatisfied

30. What three things did you find the most satisfying about the victim-offender mediation experience?

                    1. _____
                    2. _____
                    3. _____

31. What three things did you find least satisfying about the victim-of-fender mediation experience?

                    1. _____
                    2. _____
                    3. _____

THE FOLLOWING REPRESENT STATEMENTS THAT ARE SOMETIMES MADE BY OFFENDERS WHO PARTICIPATE IN VICTIM-OFFENDER MEDIATION. PLEASE INDICATE WHETHER YOU STRONGLY AGREE, AGREE, DISAGREE OR STRONGLY DISAGREE WITH EACH STATEMENT.

	STRONGLY AGREE	AGREE	DISAGREE	STRONGLY DISAGREE
32. Too much pressure was put on me to do all the talking in the meeting.				
33. I felt I had no choice about participating in the mediation session with my victim.				
34. The victim was not sincere in his/her participation.				
35. I have a better understanding of how my behavior affected the victim.				
36. The victim participated only because he/she wanted the money back.				

	STRONGLY AGREE	AGREE	DISAGREE	STRONGLY DISAGREE
37. Without the victim-offender mediation program I probably would have gone to jail.				

38. As a result of your participation in victim-offender mediation, have any of your attitudes about crime or the juvenile justice system changed?

a. yes   b. no

   38a. IF YES: What attitudes and why?

39. Of the following items, please rank the three most important concerns you have related to fairness in the justice system, with #1 being the most important.

<u>rank</u>

____ a. punishing the offender

____ b. paying back the victim

____ c. getting help for the offender

____ d. having the offender personally make things right

____ e. allowing the offender to apologize to the victim

____ f. other _____

40. Given your understanding of fairness, did you experience fairness within the justice system in your case?

a. yes   b. no

41. Is there anything else you would like to say about the mediation session with your victim or about how your case was handled?

THANK YOU VERY MUCH FOR YOUR WILLINGNESS TO PARTICIPATE IN THIS PROGRAM EVALUATION.

REFERRED-BUT-NO-MEDIATION OFFENDER
INTERVIEW SCHEDULE

Program Site: _____

Program Case Number: _____

Interview Date:_____

Interviewer: _____

Age of offender: ____

Gender: ____

Race: ____

Offense: _____

Mark Umbreit, Ph.D.
Principal Investigator
Citizens Council Mediation Services
Minnesota Citizens Council on Crime and Justice

School of Social Work
University of Minnesota

July 1992

REFERRED-BUT-NO-MEDIATION OFFENDER INTERVIEW
SCHEDULE

FIRST, I WOULD LIKE TO ASK YOU A COUPLE OF QUESTIONS
ABOUT YOUR EXPERIENCE WITH THE JUSTICE SYSTEM IN THIS
CASE.

1. How satisfied were you with the way the justice system handled your
   case?
   - a. very satisfied
   - b. satisfied
   - c. dissatisfied
   - d. very dissatisfied

2. Do you believe you were adequately held accountable
for the crime you committed?
   - a. yes   b. no

NOW I WOULD LIKE TO ASK A FEW QUESTIONS ABOUT THE VICTIM
OFFENDER MEDIATION PROGRAM THAT YOU WERE REFERRED TO.
VICTIM OFFENDER MEDIATION IS NOT SOMETHING EVERYONE
WANTS TO PARTICIPATE IN.

3. Can you tell me why you did not want to participate in the victim-offender mediation program?

4. Is there anything that might have made it easier or more tempting to
   participate in the victim-offender mediation program?

FOR EACH OF THE FOLLOWING ITEMS, PLEASE TELL ME WHETHER
THE ITEM IS VERY IMPORTANT, IMPORTANT, UNIMPORTANT OR VERY
UNIMPORTANT.

5. To be able to tell the victim what happened.

         a. very important

         b. important

         c. unimportant

         d. very unimportant

6. To compensate the victim by paying them money or doing some work.

         a. very important

         b. important

         c. unimportant

         d. very unimportant

7. To have the opportunity to work out a pay-back agreement with the victim that is acceptable to both of you.

         a. very important

         b. important

         c. unimportant

         d. very unimportant

8. To be able to apologize to the victim for what you did.

         a. very important

         b. important

         c. unimportant

         d. very unimportant

9. Do you think that a meeting with the victim might be helpful?

         a. not at all helpful

         b. somewhat helpful

         c. very helpful

10. Would you feel nervous about meeting with the victim?

         a. yes   b. no

11. Which of the following choices best describes your attitude toward the victim at this point in time?

         a. very positive

         b. positive

         c. mixed: positive and negative

         d. negative

         e. very negative

12. Which of the following choices best describes your attitude toward the idea of meeting your victim, even though you did not participate in the victim-offender mediation program?

> a. very positive
>
> b. positive
>
> c. mixed: positive and negative
>
> d. negative
>
> e. very negative

13. Do you care about what the victim thinks of you?

> a. yes   b. no

WE ARE ALMOST DONE, BUT BEFORE ENDING I WOULD LIKE TO ASK YOU A COUPLE QUESTIONS ABOUT FAIRNESS.

14. Of the following items, which is the most important to your thinking about fairness in the justice system?

> a. punishing the offender
>
> b. paying back the victim
>
> c. getting help for the offender
>
> d. having the offender personally make things right
>
> e. allowing the offender to apologize to the victim

15. Given your understanding of fairness, did you experience fairness within the justice system in your case?

> a. yes   b. no

THIS COMPLETES OUR FORMAL INTERVIEW.

16. Is there anything else you would like to say about how your case was handled by the justice system?

THANK YOU VERY MUCH FOR PARTICIPATING IN THIS PROGRAM EVALUATION.